Oracle BPM Suite 11g: Advanced BPMN Topics

Master advanced BPMN for Oracle BPM Suite including inter-process communication, handling arrays, and exception management

Mark Nelson

Tanya Williams

PUBLISHING

BIRMINGHAM - MUMBAI

Oracle BPM Suite 11g: Advanced BPMN Topics

First published: September 2012

Production Reference: 1210912

Published by Packt Publishing Ltd.
Livery Place
35 Livery Street
Birmingham B3 2PB, UK.

ISBN 978-1-84968-756-0

www.packtpub.com

Cover Image by Tina Negus (tina_manthorpe@sky.com)

Credits

Authors
Mark Nelson

Tanya Williams

Reviewers
Bhagat Nainani

Prasen Palvankar

Robert Patrick

Acquisition Editor
Stephanie Moss

Commissioning and Content Editor
Meeta Rajani

Technical Editors
Ajay Shankar

Ameya Sawant

Project Coordinator
Esha Thakker

Proofreader
Matthew Humphries

Indexer
Hemangini Bari

Graphics
Valentina Dsilva

Aditi Gajjar

Production Coordinator
Prachali Bhiwandkar

Cover Work
Prachali Bhiwandkar

About the Authors

Mark Nelson is a Consulting Solution Architect in the Oracle Fusion Middleware Architect's Team (known within the Oracle community as "the A-Team") in Oracle Development. Mark spends a significant part of his time working with Oracle BPM Suite users around the world. His other main area of technical interest currently is Continuous Integration and its application to Oracle Fusion Middleware. Mark is one of the question authors for the Oracle SOA Certification Exam. He lives in Sydney, Australia.

Tanya Williams is a Principal Solution Consultant in the Oracle Fusion Middleware Sales Consulting team in Australia. Tanya has experience helping organizations understand Oracle's products, map the product capabilities to their business needs, develop demonstrations and proofs of concept, and giving advice and guidance on adoption of Oracle products. Tanya spends much of her time working with Oracle BPM Suite and how to use Oracle BPM Suite, SOA Suite, and Service Bus to integrate with Oracle applications like E-Business Suite. Tanya has presented and run hands-on labs at Oracle OpenWorld. Tanya lives in Sydney, Australia.

Tanya and Mark contribute to the popular "RedStack" blog at `http://redstack.wordpress.com`, and have both presented at a number of Oracle OpenWorld and various regional Oracle User Group events.

Mark and Tanya would like to thank many people for their support in making this book a reality:

Stephanie, Meeta, Theresa, and all of the team at Packt Publishing for their help and support throughout this project.

Robert, Bhagat, and Prasen for their time, dedication, attention to detail, and detailed suggestions and comments.

Our respective management and colleagues for their support of this project.

All of the BPM development and product management team for their great work designing, building, and supporting Oracle BPM Suite.

And you, our readers, thank you.

About the Reviewers

Bhagat Nainani is currently Vice President of Product Development, Oracle Fusion Middleware and is responsible for product development and strategy for Business Process Management, Event Processing, and User Productivity Kit products. Over the past 18 years, he has held various technical leadership roles in database transaction processing, messaging, and middleware product groups at Oracle. He has extensive experience with SOA, process management, distributed systems, and EAI technologies. He has also contributed to many industry standards and holds six patents in distributed systems.

Bhagat holds a BS in Computer Science from Indian Institute of Technology, Varanasi (India), an MS in Computer Science from University of Texas at Austin, and an MBA from University of California, Berkeley.

Prasen Palvankar has over 25 years of experience in information technology and is currently working as a Director of Product Management at Oracle. He is responsible for outbound SOA Suite and BPM Suite product-related activities such as providing strategic support and architectural and design consultation to Oracle's SOA Suite and BPM Suite current and prospective customers. His responsibilities also include field and partner enablement, and creating and rolling out advanced deep-dive training workshops. Prasen joined Oracle in 1998 and worked as a Technical Director in the Advanced Technology Solutions group in Oracle Consulting delivering large-scale integration projects before taking on his current role as Product Management Director in 2005. Prior to joining Oracle, he worked as a Principal Software Engineer at Digital Equipment Corporation.

Prasen has co-authored books such as *Getting Started with Oracle BPM Suite 11gR1 – A Hands-On Tutorial* and *Getting Started With Oracle SOA Suite 11g R1 – A Hands-On Tutorial*.

Robert Patrick is a VP in Oracle's Fusion Middleware Development organization, responsible for a team of Solution Architects (known as the A-team) covering core middleware and integration technologies-related engagements. Robert has 19 years experience in the design and development of distributed systems, and he specializes in designing and troubleshooting large, high performance, mission-critical systems built with various middleware technologies. Prior to joining Oracle, Robert spent seven and a half years working for BEA Systems (most recently as their Deputy CTO) where he spent most of his time advising Fortune 1000 companies how to best apply middleware technology to solve their business problems. He has written papers, magazine articles, and was one of the co-authors of *Professional Oracle WebLogic Server (Wrox, 2009)* and *Mastering BEAWebLogic Server (Wiley, 2003)* as well as spoken at various industry conferences.

www.PacktPub.com

Support files, eBooks, discount offers and more

You might want to visit www.PacktPub.com for support files and downloads related to your book.

Did you know that Packt offers eBook versions of every book published, with PDF and ePub files available? You can upgrade to the eBook version at www.PacktPub.com and as a print book customer, you are entitled to a discount on the eBook copy. Get in touch with us at service@packtpub.com for more details.

At www.PacktPub.com, you can also read a collection of free technical articles, sign up for a range of free newsletters and receive exclusive discounts and offers on Packt books and eBooks.

http://PacktLib.PacktPub.com

Do you need instant solutions to your IT questions? PacktLib is Packt's online digital book library. Here, you can access, read, and search across Packt's entire library of books.

Why Subscribe?

- Fully searchable across every book published by Packt
- Copy and paste, print and bookmark content
- On demand and accessible via web browser

Free Access for Packt account holders

If you have an account with Packt at www.PacktPub.com, you can use this to access PacktLib today and view nine entirely free books. Simply use your login credentials for immediate access.

Instant Updates on New Packt Books

Get notified! Find out when new books are published by following @PacktEnterprise on Twitter, or the *Packt Enterprise* Facebook page.

This book is dedicated to Victoria.

Table of Contents

Preface   **1**

Chapter 1: Inter-process Communication   **7**

Conversations   **8**

The default conversation   10

Correlation   **11**

Correlation sets   11

Correlation when there are multiple calls   13

Throw and catch events   **14**

Send and receive tasks   **15**

When to use throw/catch events and send/receive tasks   **17**

Messages, signals, and errors   **18**

Messages   18

Signals   18

Errors   19

Invoking sub-processes   **19**

Embedded sub-processes   20

Multi-instance embedded sub-processes   21

Reusable sub-processes   22

Recommended sub-process style to use   23

Summary   **23**

Chapter 2: Inter-process Communication in Practice   **25**

Communicating between processes using messages and correlation   **25**

Communication between processes inside a loop   **35**

Communicating between processes using signals   **42**

Using reusable sub-processes   **45**

Summary   **49**

Chapter 3: Working with Arrays   51
  Data Associations   52
  Creating an empty array   53
  Creating an array with some empty elements   57
  Creating an initialized array   61
  Getting elements from arrays   62
  Setting elements in arrays   62
  Appending elements to arrays   62
  Joining two arrays   63
  Removing elements from arrays   63
  Iterating over arrays with a multi-instance embedded sub-process   63
    Cardinality or collection   64
    Sequential or parallel   65
    Using a completion condition   65
    Scope   65
  Practice: Iterating over an array using an embedded sub-process   66
  Summary   68

Chapter 4: Handling Exceptions   69
  Mechanisms for catching exceptions in BPMN   70
    Boundary events   70
      Event sub-processes   71
  Exception propagation with sub-processes and peer processes   73
    Exception propagation with embedded sub-processes   73
    Exception propagation with sub-processes invoked with a call activity   75
    Exception propagation with peer processes invoked with a throw event   75
    Exception propagation with peer processes invoked with a send task   76
  How BPM exceptions affect the SCA composite   76
  Summary   76

Chapter 5: Handling Exceptions in Practice   77
  Using boundary events to implement timeouts   77
  Using boundary events to implement the cancel message use case   79
  Using event sub-processes   84
  Propagating exceptions using peer processes   88
  Summary   90

Index   93

Preface

Welcome to *Oracle BPM Suite 11g: Advanced BPMN Topics*. This book brings you concise and focused information on key topics about Oracle BPM Suite, in a small, easy to digest format.

Being about advanced topics, we assume that you are already familiar with Oracle BPM Suite and with BPMN in general. We will not take time to explain common tasks like how to model a BPMN process in JDeveloper, or how to access the implementation properties for a task in a process, for example. We assume that you already know how to do these kinds of tasks. If you do not, you might want to consider reading some of Packt's other great Oracle BPM Suite titles such as *Getting Started with Oracle BPM Suite 11gR1* or *Oracle BPM Suite Cookbook* to learn these skills.

In particular, we assume that you are familiar with the following concepts:

- Process
- Process instance
- Task/Activity
- Event
- Throw/catch
- Exception
- Embedded sub-process
- Event sub-process
- Business object
- Data association
- Composite

We also assume that you are familiar with the basic operation of JDeveloper and that you know how to use the component palette, access properties, access various views, and deploy processes. We also assume that you know how to use Enterprise Manager start test instances and review the audit trail of these instances.

We focus on BPMN topics that we have seen, through our experience, that people have difficulty in understanding and applying. For each topic, we will present some theory and background information, and then a number of practical examples to help you to practice what you have learned in the theory chapters.

What this book covers

Chapter 1, Inter-process Communication introduces us to the theory of how processes can communicate with each other and with other components. A number of topics are covered such as: conversations—what they are, the default and advanced conversations. We discuss correlation—automatic and message based, correlation sets and keys, and correlation inside loops and when there are multiple calls. Throw and catch events, send and receive tasks, and when to use each are examined. We compare messages, signals, and errors. Sub-processes are explored—embedded, multi-instance, and reusable, and when to use each.

Chapter 2, Inter-process Communication in Practice presents a series of practical exercises to help you to explore the theory present in *Chapter 1, Inter-process Communication* . The examples include communicating between processes using messages and correlation, using correlation inside loops, communication between processes using signals, and reusable sub-processes.

Chapter 3, Working with Arrays presents both theory and several practical exercises on handling arrays in BPM. Topics include data association, creating an empty array, creating an array with empty elements, creating an initialized array, getting an element from an array, setting an element in an array, appending elements to an array, joining arrays, removing elements from an array, and iterating over arrays—cardinality and collections, sequential and parallel, completion conditions, and scope.

Chapter 4, Handling Exceptions discusses the theory behind handling exceptions in BPM. Topics include business and system exceptions, boundary events, event sub-processes, exception propagation with embedded sub-processes, call, throw and send, and how BPM exceptions affect the SCA composite.

Chapter 5, Handling Exceptions in Practice will guide us through a number of practical examples that help to reinforce the theory in *Chapter 4, Handling Exceptions*. The examples include implementing a timeout use case with boundary events, implementing a "cancel message" use case, using event sub-processes, and exploring exception propagation in peer processes.

What you need for this book

To run the examples in the book, the following software will be required. You may choose to either download and install the software yourself, or to download a pre-built VM with the software already installed for you.

If you choose to install your own environment, you will need the following:

- Oracle BPM server: Oracle BPM Suite 11.1.1.5 with "Feature Pack" patch applied, or a later release. You will need to download both the BPM installer and the Repository Creation Utility. Please refer to the documentation if you are not familiar with the installation process.

- Pre-requisites for BPM: Oracle WebLogic Server 10.3.5 or later must be the correct version for the version of BPM that you are using — the last digit, for example, 5 must match. Note that release 12.1.1 or later is not compatible with BPM at the time of writing.

- An Oracle Database — you can use the free Oracle 10g Express Edition. Please be sure to read the installion guide to make sure you have the correct database settings before you start the installation.

- Java Development Kit 1.6.30 or later (1.7 is also acceptable).

- Oracle JDeveloper: Oracle JDeveloper 11.1.1.5 with "Feature Pack" patch applied, or a later release. You need to install the SOA and BPM plugins from the Update Center (choose Help/Check for Updates). Note that the JDeveloper version must be exactly the same as the Oracle BPM Suite version. Note that release 11.1.2.0 or later is not compatible with BPM at the time of writing.

If you prefer to download a VM with all of the software already installed, you can download a VM from Oracle at the following address:

http://www.oracle.com/technetwork/middleware/soasuite/learnmore/vmsoa-172279.html

Where to download the software from

BPM Suite:

http://www.oracle.com/technetwork/middleware/bpm/downloads/index.html

WebLogic:

http://www.oracle.com/technetwork/middleware/weblogic/downloads/index.html

Database:

```
http://www.oracle.com/technetwork/products/express-edition/downloads/
index.html
```

JDK:

```
http://www.oracle.com/technetwork/java/javase/downloads/index.html
```

JDeveloper:

```
http://www.oracle.com/technetwork/developer-tools/jdev/downloads/
index.html
```

Conventions

In this book, you will find a number of styles of text that distinguish between different kinds of information. Here are some examples of these styles, and an explanation of their meaning.

Code words in text are shown as follows: "Set the value of the expression to work. number * work.number".

A block of code is set as follows:

```xml
<?xml version="1.0" encoding="UTF-8" ?>
<xsd:schema xmlns:xsd="http://www.w3.org/2001/XMLSchema"
  xmlns:ns="http://www.example.org"
  targetNamespace="http://www.example.org"
  elementFormDefault="qualified">
  <xsd:complexType name="TElement">
    <xsd:sequence>
      <xsd:element name="user" type="xsd:string"/>
      <xsd:element name="outcome" type="xsd:string"/>
    </xsd:sequence>
  </xsd:complexType>
</xsd:schema>
```

New terms and **important words** are shown in bold. Words that you see on the screen, in menus or dialog boxes for example, appear in the text like this: "Switch to the source editor using the **Source** tab at the bottom of the editor."

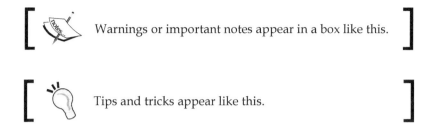

Warnings or important notes appear in a box like this.

Tips and tricks appear like this.

Reader feedback

Feedback from our readers is always welcome. Let us know what you think about this book—what you liked or may have disliked. Reader feedback is important for us to develop titles that you really get the most out of.

To send us general feedback, simply send an e-mail to feedback@packtpub.com, and mention the book title through the subject of your message.

If there is a topic that you have expertise in and you are interested in either writing or contributing to a book, see our author guide on www.packtpub.com/authors.

Customer support

Now that you are the proud owner of a Packt book, we have a number of things to help you to get the most from your purchase.

Errata

Although we have taken every care to ensure the accuracy of our content, mistakes do happen. If you find a mistake in one of our books—maybe a mistake in the text or the code—we would be grateful if you would report this to us. By doing so, you can save other readers from frustration and help us improve subsequent versions of this book. If you find any errata, please report them by visiting http://www.packtpub.com/support, selecting your book, clicking on the **errata submission form** link, and entering the details of your errata. Once your errata are verified, your submission will be accepted and the errata will be uploaded to our website, or added to any list of existing errata, under the Errata section of that title.

Piracy

Piracy of copyright material on the Internet is an ongoing problem across all media. At Packt, we take the protection of our copyright and licenses very seriously. If you come across any illegal copies of our works, in any form, on the Internet, please provide us with the location address or website name immediately so that we can pursue a remedy.

Please contact us at `copyright@packtpub.com` with a link to the suspected pirated material.

We appreciate your help in protecting our authors, and our ability to bring you valuable content.

Questions

You can contact us at `questions@packtpub.com` if you are having a problem with any aspect of the book, and we will do our best to address it.

1
Inter-process Communication

Welcome to our exploration of some of the advanced topics in BPMN. When we set out to write this book, we chose the areas where we see the most confusion and difficulty in understanding how to use BPMN. Over the next five chapters, we will look at how process instances can communicate, how exceptions are handled and propagated, and how to deal with data in arrays. We will present theory and also build practical exercises together so that you can see how the theory is applied. Let's start our journey by building an understanding of inter-process communication.

Inter-process communication refers to the ability for **instances** of processes to communicate with other instances of the same process, with instances of other processes, and with services. Such communication is usually implemented so that process instances can work collaboratively to achieve a given goal. Common scenarios when this may occur include:

- When common logic is extracted from a number of processes into a reusable "utility" process
- When the occurrence of an event in one process means that another, perhaps separate, process needs to be started — this is often seen where the second process is an audit or investigation process
- Where a process has a set of data, needs to run a common set of logic over each item in that data set, and then consolidate the results
- Through normal decomposition of a business process into various levels of granularity, resulting in the need for the process to invoke one or more sub-processes to accomplish its work

There are different mechanisms available for processes to communicate with each other. In this chapter, we will explore the options and when we should employ each.

Conversations

A **conversation** is a set of message exchanges. The message exchanges can be **synchronous** or **asynchronous**, but they should all be about the same subject matter, for example, a particular order, customer, case, and so on. The set of messages that forms the conversation is typically a request and a response, or a request and several (possible) responses.

[A single process instance can participate in more than one conversation simultaneously.]

The **collaboration diagram** allows you to visualize the process in the context of its conversations. You can access the collaboration diagram using the **Collaboration Diagram** tab at the bottom of the process editor in JDeveloper. An example of a collaboration diagram is shown in the following diagram:

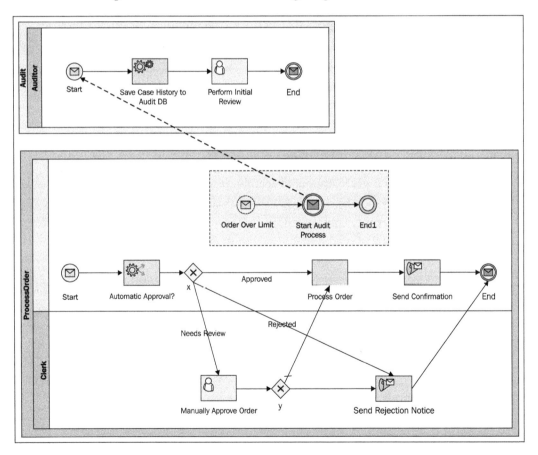

This example includes a number of features that will be discussed in this book. The small, disconnected process that begins with `Order Over Limit` is an **event sub-process**. These will be discussed in detail in *Chapter 4, Handling Exceptions*. Briefly, they are invoked if a particular **event** (set of circumstances) occurs at any time during the execution of the process they belong to, the `ProcessOrder` process in this example. If at any time it is determined that the order is over some predefined limit, then an audit is required. The event sub-process sends a message to start the `Audit` process using a **throw message event**, which we will discuss later in this chapter. The collaboration diagram allows us to see both of the processes that are involved in this collaboration and shows us visually where the interaction between them occurs (with the dotted arrow from the **throw message event** to the start of the `Audit` process).

Conversations may also be **scoped**; this means that they may be defined in a smaller scope than the process as a whole. For example, you can define a conversation inside an **embedded sub-process**. To define a scoped conversation, you must do so in the **Structure** pane so that the conversation is placed in the correct scope. If you do not define the conversation in the **Structure** pane, it will inherit the process scope. The following image shows a process with two conversations defined: `myconv1` at the process (global) scope, and the scoped conversation `scopeConv`, which is inside an embedded sub-process:

In addition to defining conversations for communication with other processes, each **service** that you want to interact with will also require a conversation. When implementing your process, you need to create a conversation for each service, choose **Service Call** as the type, and then select the service you wish to interact with.

The default conversation

Each process has a **default conversation**. The default conversation is used to expose services provided by the process, and it therefore controls the interface for invocation of the process. This interface manifests itself as the WSDL port type.

The default conversation can be defined "top down" by starting with WSDL (**service contract**) for the process and creating the conversation from that, or "bottom up" by defining the arguments for the process and having the service interface (WSDL) generated from the process.

If we are using the bottom-up approach, the interface is defined by adding arguments to the start node, as shown in the following screenshot. You need to select **Define Interface** as the message exchange type to use the bottom-up approach. The arguments can have simple types (String, Date, Integer, and so on) or complex types, that is, they can be based on the **business object** (which in turn can be based on an element or type definition in an XSD).

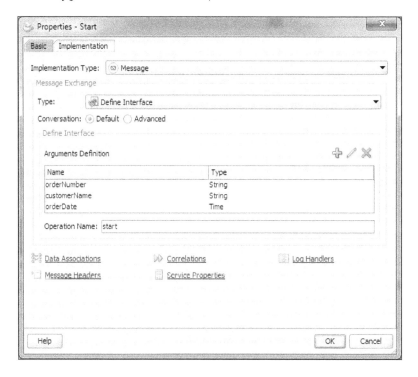

Correlation

Correlation is the mechanism that is used to associate a message with the conversation that it belongs to. There are two main classes of correlation:

- **Automatic correlation** refers to mechanisms where the correlation is handled automatically. BPM uses mechanisms like WS-Addressing and JMS Message IDs to achieve automatic correlation.
- **Message-based correlation** refers to the mechanism the process developer needs to define some **keys**, which can be extracted from the message in order to determine which conversation a message belongs to. Examples are given in the next section.

There are some occasions when message-based correlation is necessary because automatic correlation is not available, for example:

- When the other participant does not support WS-addressing, or
- When a participant joins the conversation part way through but has only the data values, but no other information about the conversation

If you do not specify any settings for message-based correlation, the runtime engine will attempt to use automatic correlation. If it is not possible to do so, then you will get a **correlation fault**. The engine checks to see if the called process or service supports WS-addressing, in which case it will insert a WS-addressing header into the call. It will then wait for a matching reply. Similarly, if JMS is being used to transport the message, it will look for a reply message with the JMS correlation ID that matches the JMS message ID of the message it sent.

Correlation is especially important inside a **loop** construct, as there may be multiple threads/receives waiting at once, and the engine needs a way to know which reply belongs with which receive.

Correlation sets

When using message-based correlation, you define a set of keys that are used to determine which conversation a message belongs to. This set of keys is called a **correlation set**.

A correlation set is a list of the (minimum) set of attributes that are needed to uniquely identify the conversation. An example of a correlation set may be `orderNumber` plus `customerNumber`.

When the runtime engine sees a conversation that uses message-based correlation, which has a correlation set attached to the start activity, it will create an **MD5 hash** from the values of the correlation keys and use that to identify the correct reply message if and when it arrives.

When you are using **message-based correlation**, only the **called process** needs to be aware of correlation, not the **calling process**. The runtime engine will take care of details for the calling process, so you do not need to include any correlation details in the process model for the calling process.

 It is important to understand that these rules do not apply when the calling process wants to call the called process more than once, as is the case when the call is inside a loop, for example. This scenario will be discussed shortly.

In the called process, you need to include the correlation set definition, and specify that the appropriate **events** or **tasks** use correlation. Let's look at an example in the following diagram:

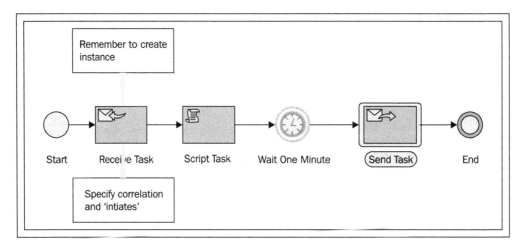

The **receive task** in this process has correlation specified in its properties. It has a correlation set identified, which contains a single key called `ck_number`, and the mode is set to **Initiates** as shown in the following screenshot. This tells the runtime engine that this process instance is going to use message-based correlation. It also has the **Create Instance** property set. This tells the runtime engine that an inbound message will start an instance of this process.

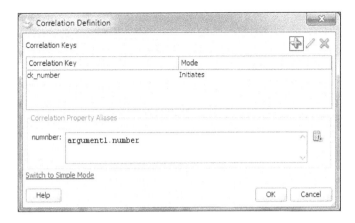

If there are other **receive tasks** or **message catch events** in this process, they need to have correlation defined with the same correlation set and the mode set to **Uses**. These are called **mid-point receives** — places where the process instance can receive another message after it has already started executing. These could be used by the calling process to send a "cancel" message to tell the running instance of the called process to stop work, for example.

You do not need to define any correlation properties on the outputs of the process, for example its **send task**, or any **end (message) nodes** or **throw message events**. Only inputs have correlation properties defined.

Correlation when there are multiple calls

There are some occasions when you will want to call a service or process several times from the same **instance** of a process. This commonly occurs when you want to call the service for every item in a collection, for example.

In this scenario, you need to place the send task and receive task (or throw and catch events) inside an embedded sub-process and define a **scoped conversation** inside the embedded sub-process. As mentioned previously, you will not need to define correlation information in the calling process, just the called process.

Here is an example of a process that contains a multi-instance embedded sub-process that iterates over an array of input data, calling another process to carry out some work on each element in that array, in parallel.

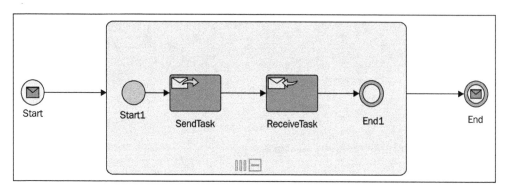

There is a scoped conversation defined inside the embedded sub-process as we see in the following image. The send and receive tasks each use this conversation, rather than the default conversation. We will build this process in the next chapter.

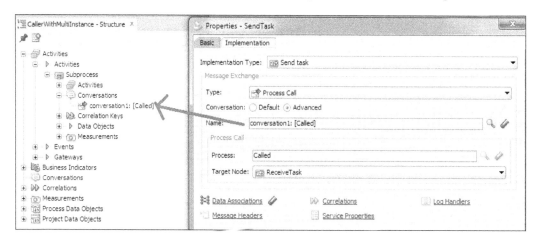

Throw and catch events

Throw and **catch** events provide a mechanism to communicate with another process or service. Specifically, you can use throw events to invoke:

- Another BPMN process
- A BPEL process
- An adapter

- A mediator that is exposed as a service
- Any other component that is exposed as a service

Throw events are usually asynchronous. As soon as the throw event is executed, the process continues with the next task. It does not wait for a response. It is possible for a throw event to be synchronous, in the sense that you can invoke a synchronous service with a throw event and it can reply on the same connection—as opposed to sending a callback later. You can specify that you want to wait for a synchronous reply using the **Synchronous** property on the throw event. If you want to invoke a synchronous service or process, you could alternatively use a **service task**.

It is also important to understand that processes invoked through throw/catch events (and also those invoked through send/receive tasks) are not **child processes** of the invoking process, they are **peers**. This will be important later on when we discuss **exception handling**.

You can throw a message or a signal using a throw event. Throwing a message is the equivalent of sending a SOAP message to a service. Throwing a signal is the equivalent of publishing an event into the event delivery network. You can use a throw event to invoke a process that starts with a receive task, but only if that receive task has the **Create New Instance** property set.

Send and receive tasks

The **send task** allows you to send a message to a receive task in another process, and the **receive task** allows you to receive a message from a send task in another process. The send task is similar to the throw message event; however, you cannot use the send task to invoke a process that starts with a message start event. There are no send and receive tasks for signals, only for messages. Send and receive tasks also allow you to attach **boundary events** (which will be discussed in *Chapter 4, Handling Exceptions*) to them. This is an important difference.

You can use the receive task to start a process, however, in this case, you must set the **Create Instance** property and there must be a single start node of type "none" immediately before the receive task.

The following diagram shows three processes that use the methods we have discussed to communicate with each other. The dotted arrows indicate where throw and catch message events are used by Process3 to invoke Process1, and by Process1 to return some data to Process3 when it is finished. The red arrows indicate where send and receive message tasks are used by Process1 to invoke Process2, and by Process2 to return some data to Process1 when it is finished.

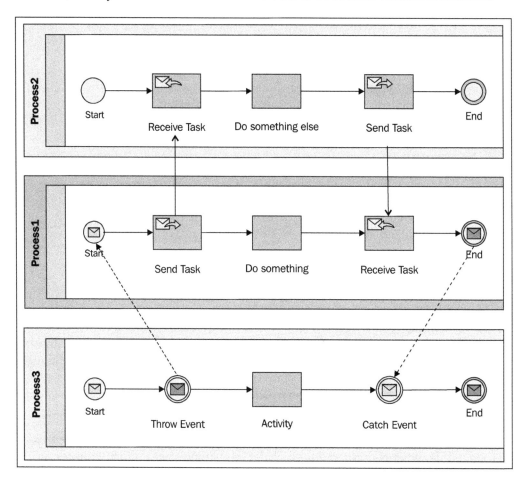

Let us consider what happens when an instance of Process3 is executed:

1. Process3 starts.
2. Process3 throws a message event to start Process1.
3. Right away, Process3 goes on to Activity.

4. At the same time (more or less,) `Process1` starts.

5. `Process1` sends a message to start `Process2`.

6. Right away, `Process1` goes on to `Do something`.

7. At the same time (more or less), `Process2` starts.

8. `Process2` goes on to `Do something else`.

9. While all of this is going on, when `Process3` finished doing `Activity`, it went on to `CatchEvent` and paused there waiting for a response back from `Process1`.

10. Similarly, when `Process1` finished `Do something`, it went on to `ReceiveTask` and paused there waiting for a response back from `Process2`.

11. When `Process2` finished `Do something else`, it sent a response (in this case by sending a message) back to `Process1`.

12. `Process1` wakes up upon receiving a response (message) from `Process2` and then sends its response (by throwing a message event) back to `Process3`.

13. `Process3` wakes up upon receiving a response (catching a message event) from `Process1` and then moves on to its end.

When to use throw/catch events and send/receive tasks

The following table is a quick guide to which kind of inter-process communication mechanism you should use in various circumstances:

	Throw/catch message events	Throw/catch signal events	Send/receive tasks
Ability to attach a boundary event to catch errors	No	No	Yes
Asynchronous	Either	Yes	Yes
Invoked process becomes a …	Child	Child	Peer
The process you want to invoke starts with a …	Catch message event or receive task that creates an instance	Catch signal event	Receive task

	Throw/catch message events	Throw/catch signal events	Send/receive tasks
You know who the receiver is at design time	Yes	No	Yes
You want to send the 'message' to ... receivers	One	Any number	One
Failure of called process propagates to calling process*	No	No	Yes

 Propagation of failures will be covered in *Chapter 4, Handling Exceptions*.

Messages, signals, and errors

Throw and catch events come in several types including messages, signals, and errors. Let us consider these different types and when we might use each.

Messages

A **message** is a set of data based on some type definition (a data structure), which is sent from a sender to a receiver. The sender knows who the receiver is and addresses the message to the receiver. If the message cannot be delivered, the sender is informed and can then take the appropriate action, for example, they might retry sending the message later. In the context of the runtime environment, a message is a SOAP message sent from a service consumer to a service provider (or vice versa). The type definition is normally placed in an XSD for easy reuse, however, it may be in a WSDL file. It will often be in a WSDL file for pre-existing services.

Signals

A **signal** is a set of data, based on some type definition, which is broadcast from a sender and enters the **Event Delivery Network** as an event. If there are any **subscribers** for that particular type of event, the EDN will (most likely) deliver the event to them. We say "most likely" because the EDN does not offer the same guarantees about delivery as, for example, SOAP over JMS does.

The EDN does allow you to configure **once and only once** delivery, which is transactional—it is delivered in a global transaction—but it is not possible to create a durable subscriber. This means that if there is a system failure, signals may be lost and may not be delivered when the system is restarted.

Neither rollback nor retry mechanisms are provided by the EDN—except in the case of once and only once delivery. For this reason, signals are normally used when delivery is time sensitive and it no longer matters if a signal was delivered after a certain period of time has passed. The signal's type definition is also in XSD. Note that the sender (broadcaster) does not know whether there are any receivers (subscribers), how many there are, and whether the signals are ever delivered to them.

 The **Event Delivery Network** is a feature of the Oracle BPM Suite that provides a mechanism to publish events and optionally take various actions on them, such as pattern matching and to subscribe to events so that they will be delivered to the subscriber when they are generated. An in-depth discussion of its capabilities is beyond the scope of this volume.

Errors

Errors are exceptions. These would normally manifest as SOAP faults in the runtime environment. Exceptions are discussed in detail in *Chapter 5, Handling Exceptions in Practice*.

Invoking sub-processes

There are two methods available to invoke a sub-process—the **embedded sub-process** and the **reusable sub-process**. The embedded sub-process also contains a special case called the **multi-instance embedded sub-process**, which as the name suggests, allows us to run multiple instances of the embedded sub-process. Let us take a look at the differences and when we might use each.

Embedded sub-processes

An embedded sub-process is included in the same process model as its parent process. It is, in fact, included in the flow of the parent process. The embedded sub-process can be **expanded** to show its contents, or **collapsed**, in which case it is shown as a single task in the parent process as we can see in the following diagram:

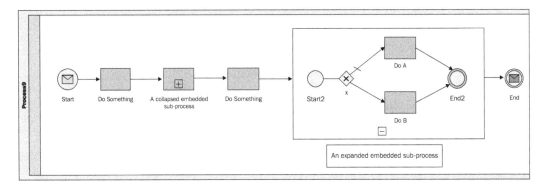

Embedded sub-processes provide a number of capabilities that make them useful:

- They establish **scope** for conversations, variables, and exceptions. This means that we can define a conversation or a variable inside an embedded sub-process and it will only be visible inside that embedded sub-process. This is particularly useful if we need to deal with a large amount of data for a short time during the process. By placing that data in variables that are scoped (defined) inside an embedded sub-process, we will only force the runtime environment to persist them while the embedded sub-process is running, thereby improving performance and minimizing our storage needs.

- They also set the **boundary** for exceptions. We can attach boundary events to an embedded sub-process (these will be discussed in detail in *Chapter 4, Handling Exceptions*) so that we can localize the exception handling for anything that goes wrong during the embedded sub-process. This can be useful if we want to be able to catch an error and then retry the logic inside the embedded sub-process. In this case, you can think of the embedded sub-process as being similar to the try/catch structure in many common programming language environments.

- Embedded sub-processes can see and manipulate their parent's variables, unlike reusable sub-processes.

- Embedded sub-processes can be placed inside each other to create hierarchies of scopes, each with their own variables, conversations, and exception handling if desired.

- They provide a mechanism to **loop** or repeat. You can specify an arbitrary number of times to repeat, or you can use an expression to calculate how many times to repeat the embedded sub-process. These expressions are able to reference variables and can also use XPath functions. You can evaluate the expression before or after the loop execution, giving you the equivalent of do...while and while semantics. You can also set a maximum number of iterations to prevent infinite loops.

- They also provide a mechanism that **iterates** over a collection, which is discussed in the next section.

Multi-instance embedded sub-processes

The multi-instance embedded sub-process is a special case that allows you to iterate over a **collection** of data. This will be covered in detail in *Chapter 3, Working with Arrays*, but for now let's discuss the main characteristics of the multi-instance embedded sub-process:

- The multiple instances can be run sequentially (one after the other) or in parallel.

- You can specify how many instances to run at runtime based on the **cardinality** of an object (like an array) or by iterating over a **collection**. Loops based on cardinality resemble a for loop, while those based on a collection resemble a foreach loop.

- You can additionally specify a **completion condition** so that you are able to "short circuit" the iteration if you find that you are finished before all of the iterations are complete. This may be the case, for example, when you are searching for a single item in the collection that you want to do something to or with. Once you find that item, it is no longer necessary to continue iterating over the rest of the collection.

Multi-instance embedded sub-processes also share the characteristics of "normal" embedded sub-processes. They establish scope for conversations, variables, and exception handling, can be placed inside each other, and can access their parent's variables.

An interesting case to consider is iteration over lists of lists. Using a multi-instance embedded sub-process you can iterate over the items in the outer list in parallel, while a second multi-instance embedded sub-process iterates over the items in the inner list, which is the current element of the outer list sequentially.

A good example of when this might happen is performing pathology tests. Often a series of tests can be performed one after the other on a single sample, but other tests require different samples. If there were n series of tests to be performed, this could be represented as a list of lists and modeled in this fashion.

This is illustrated in the following process model, which also includes a final review and possible repeating of one or more series of tests:

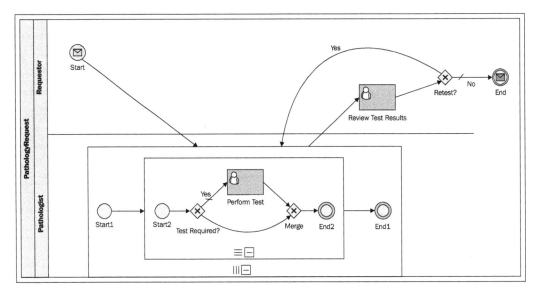

Reusable sub-processes

Reusable sub-processes are included in the same project as their parent process(es), but in a separate process model. They must start with a **catch none event** and end with a **throw none event**.

Any process in the same project (**composite**) as the reusable sub-process is able to call the reusable sub-process, however, they are not exposed as services, they are not shown in composite, and there is no way to invoke them directly from outside of the composite in which they are defined. Additionally, at runtime a reusable sub-process is shown as executing inline, within the outer process flow—the process that invoked it—even though it was modeled in a separate process model.

Reusable sub-processes are invoked using the **call** activity. Variables of the parent (calling) process are not available to the reusable sub-process unless you pass them to the reusable sub-process as **arguments**.

Recommended sub-process style to use

The following table is a quick guide to which kind of sub-process you should use in various circumstances.

	Embedded	Multi-instance	Reusable
Want access to parent's variables	Yes	Yes	Must pass them
Need looping	Yes	No	No*
Need to iterate over a collection	No	Yes	No*
Need to call it from more than one parent	No	No	Yes
Want parallel execution	No	Yes	No*
Want to establish a new scope	Yes	Yes	Yes
Want short-circuit completion	No	Yes	No*

 The scenarios marked with asterisks in the preceding table can be achieved using a reusable sub-process, but you must do a bit more of the work yourself if you choose that approach — you will need to explicitly model things such as looping into your parent process.

Summary

In this chapter, we have seen how to use send and receive tasks and throw and catch events to enable inter-process communication. We have explored the important role that conversations and correlation play in ensuring that replies are delivered to the correct instances, and even threads within instances. We have also considered when to use different kinds of inter-process communication options and when to use different kinds of processes.

In the next chapter, we will put this new knowledge into practice by building a number of example processes to demonstrate inter-process communication to ourselves in action.

2
Inter-process Communication in Practice

In the previous chapter, we learned about the various approaches to inter-process communication including send and receive tasks, and throw and catch events. We also discussed important concepts like conversations and correlation.

In this chapter, we will put this theory into practice by building a number of examples to consolidate our knowledge. When you have finished each practical exercise, we encourage you to experiment further — make some changes and see what happens.

Communicating between processes using messages and correlation

In this practice activity, we will build two processes and call one from the other using **correlation**. The example that we will use is illustrated in the following diagram. We will create a **calling process** that will send a number to the **called process**. The called process will square the number (multiply it by itself) and return the result to the calling process.

We will run multiple instances of the calling process, which will start multiple instances of the called process—one each. We will observe that the correct result is returned to each instance of the calling process.

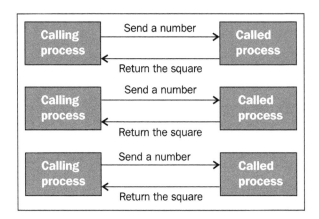

1. Start by creating a new BPM Application in JDeveloper. Name both the application and the project as **Practice1**.

2. Choose the option to create an empty composite

    Let's define the data structures that we will use in this project. For this practice activity, we will create a business object called **Work** that will hold both the number and its square.

3. Open **BPM Process Navigator**, expand the navigation tree, and create a new **Module** in **Business Catalog**. Name it as **Data**.

4. Now create a **Business Object** in that module named **Work**. Add two attributes named number and square, both of type Int.

5. Your project should now look similar to the following screenshot:

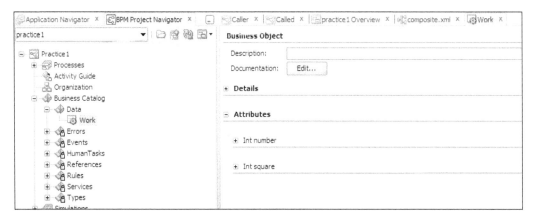

Next, we will create the called process.

6. Create a new **Process** and name it **Called**.

7. Choose the **Reusable Process** type. This will create an empty process with a start node and an end node, both of type `None`.

8. Between the start and end nodes, add the following:

    ○ A receive task

    ○ A script task

    ○ A timer catch event

    ○ A send task

Your process should now look similar to the following diagram:

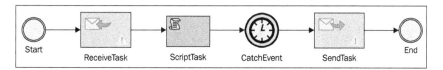

9. Create a process data object named **work** of type `<Component>` and choose your `Data.Work` **Business Object**. We will use this to store the data we are working on inside the process instance.

10. Open the properties for **ReceiveTask** and go to the **Implementation** tab.

11. Check the **Create Instance** checkbox so that a new instance of the process will be created when a message is received by this task.

12. Set **Message Exchange Type** to **Define Interface** and add an argument named **argument1** of type `<Component>` and choose **Data.Work**.

13. Click on **Data Associations** and map `argument1` to `work` so that the data passed in to the process in `ReceiveTask` will be stored in our process data object `work`:

The **Properties - ReceiveTask** screen should now look similar to the following screenshot:

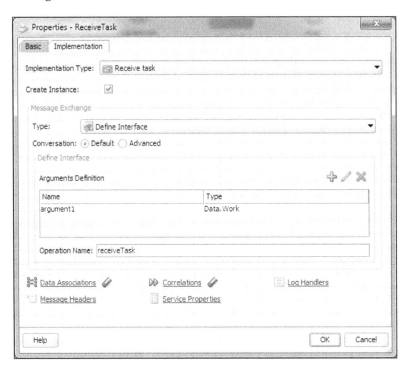

Let's recap what we have just done. We have a receive task that receives a message from some other process. This message contains data of the type Data.Work. We defined that earlier. This has two integers in it—one to hold number and one to hold that number's square. When a message is received we will start a new instance of this process.

Later, we are going to use number in the input message as the **correlation key**. When this process instance is finished it sends a reply message. BPM will deliver this reply to the process instance that called this process with the same number in the message that it originally sent. The number is our correlation key—the data that uniquely identifies the conversation that this process instance belongs to. Now, let's implement the logic to calculate the square:

1. Open the properties for **ScriptTask** and go to the **Implementation** tab.

2. Open the Data Associations editor and set the value of **work.square** on the right-hand side of the screen to **expression** (you can drag the little calculator icon and drop it on **work.square**).

3. Set the value of **expression** to **work.number * work.number**.

Your data associations should look similar to the following screenshot:

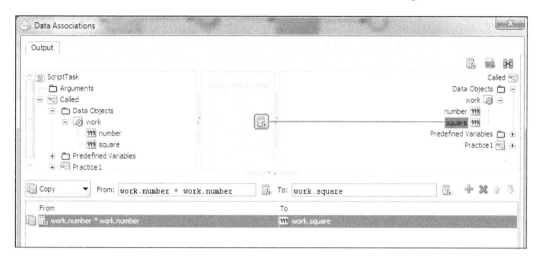

This will calculate the square of input `number` and store it in the `square` field in our process data object.

The next activity, the **timer catch event**, is just there to slow the process down. We want it to be in the "running" state long enough so that we will have the time to look at it while it is still executing, and be able to create a number of instances that will all be running at the same time.

1. Open the properties for the timer catch event and go to the **Implementation** tab.

2. Set **Time Cycle** to one minute. Note that the last three numbers are in the format `hour:minute:second`:

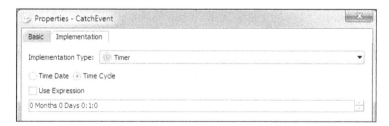

Fnally, let's set up the send task to return our results to the caller:

1. Open its properties and go to the **Implementation** tab.

2. Set **Message Exchange Type** to **Define Interface**. Add an argument named **output1** of type `<Component>` and choose **Data.Work**.

3. Click on **Data Associations** and map the `work` process data object to `output1`.

    Your properties should now look similar to the following screenshot:

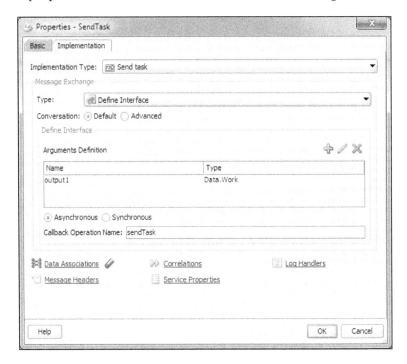

    That completes the `Called` proces.

Now, let's create another process that will call this process:

1. Create a second process called `Caller`. Choose the **Type** as **Asynchronous Service**. This will create a new process with start and end nodes of type `Message`.

2. Add the following to your process:
    ○   SendTask
    ○   ReceiveTask

    Your process should look similar to the following diagram:

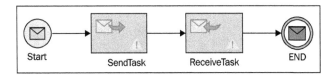

We will use `SendTask` to invoke the called process, and `ReceiveTask` to receive the reply:

3. Create a process data object named `work` of type `Data.Work`.

4. Open the **Implementation** tab for **Start** and add an argument named **argument1** of **Type** as **Data.Work**.

5. Open **Data Associations** and map `argument1` to `work`.

   Your properties should look similar to the following screenshot:

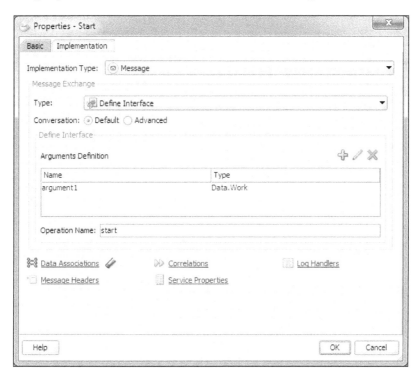

6. Open the **Implementation** tab for **SendTask**.

7. Set **Message Exchange Type** to **Process Call**. Choose the **Process:** as **Called** and its **Target Node:** as **ReceiveTask**.

8. Open **Data Associations** and map `work` to `argument1`.

9. Click on **Correlations** then add a new property (using the add icon in the top-right corner of the dialog box) called `number`.

10. Check the **Initiates** checkbox to tell BPM that this is the first message in the conversation — the one where we need to set up correlation. Map the `number` property to the `number` attribute in `argument1`.

Your properties should look similar to the following screenshot:

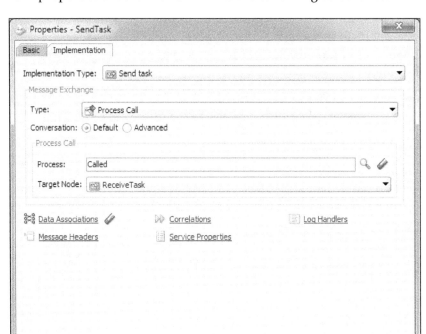

11. Open the **Implementation** tab for **ReceiveTask**.

12. Set **Message Exchange Type** to **Process Call**.

13. Choose the **Called** process and set its **Target Node** as SendTask.

14. Open **Data Associations** and map output1 to work.

15. Click on **Correlations** and then select the **number** property.

16. Do not check the **Initiates** checkbox (this sets **Mode** to **Uses**) to tell BPM that this is the reply message in the conversation. Map the number property to the number attribute in output1. You can click on **Switch to Advanced Mode** to confirm that **Mode** is set to **Uses**.

Your properties should look similar to the following screenshot:

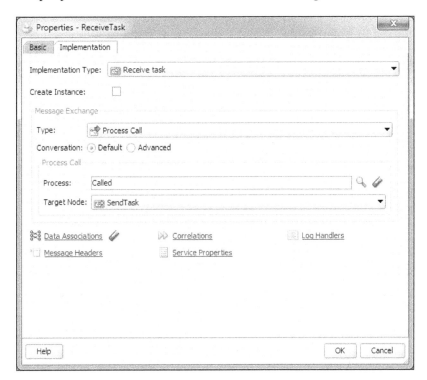

Deploy the composite to your server and start some test instances. Start three instances with the inputs as follows:

Instance	Number	Square
1	1	0
2	2	0
3	3	0

Within the minute that these process instances will run for, you can go and look at the instances in Enterprise Manager to see what they are doing. For each one, you should be able to see the Caller process instance send a message that is received by a new instance of the Called process. You should see the Called process calculate the square and then wait for its one minute timer to expire.

The following screenshot is an example of what you should see in Enterprise Manager:

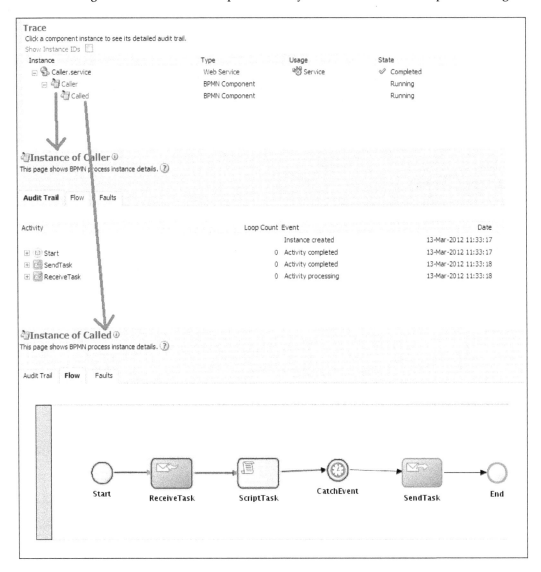

Now, wait until your instances are completed and check that each one has received the correct reply message. You can check this by checking that the `square` field in the output of `ReceiveTask` in the `Caller` process contains the correct number. Here is an example:

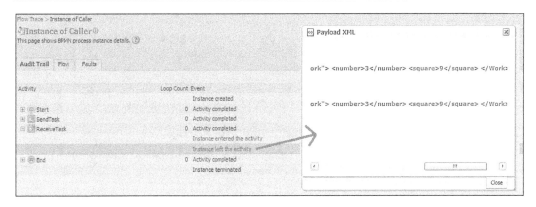

This practice activity has shown us how to use correlation and **default conversation** to communicate between instances of processes. We have seen that each of the instances of the `Caller` process started a conversation with an instance of the `Called` process, and each reply was sent back to the correct caller.

Communication between processes inside a loop

In this practice activity, we will extend the previous activity to include correlation when we call the `Called` process multiple times inside a loop. This will allow us to explore a slightly different area of correlation—**scoped conversations** and correlation when the process is participating in multiple conversations. In this activity, our `Calling` process starts a number of **sub-processes**. Each of these in turn starts an instance of the called process, as illustrated in the following diagram:

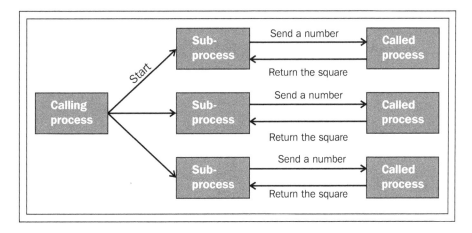

You need to complete the first practice activity before starting this one. This activity will extend the project we created previously.

Let's start by creating some additional data types we will need now:

1. Create a second **Business Object** called **WorkArray**.

2. Add a single attribute named **work** of type <Array> of **<Component>** Work. We will use this to hold our list of input data.

3. Create another process called **CallerWithMultiInstance**, again choosing the **Asynchronous Service** type.

4. Add an embedded sub-process to your process — be careful to choose the **Subprocess** activity, and not **Event Subprocess**. Add **SendTask** and a **ReceiveTask** inside the sub-process. Your process should now look similar to the following screenshot:

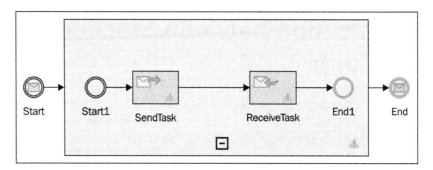

5. Create a new process data object called **workArray** of type <Component> and **Data.WorkArray**.

6. Open the **Implementation** tab for the **Start** node. Add an argument named **argument1** of **Type** as **Data.WorkArray**.

7. Open **Data Associations** and map argument1 to workArray.

Your properties should look similar to the following screenshot:

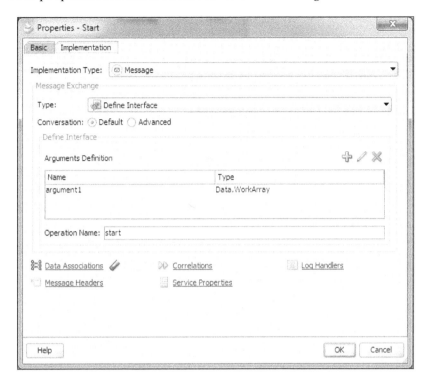

8. Open **Properties - Subprocess** and open the **Loop Characteristics** tab. Select **MultiInstance** as the type of loop.

9. Set **Mode** to **Parallel**. Set **Creation Type** to **Collection**.

10. Click on the pencil icon in **Loop Data Input** and create an argument called **loopDataInput** of type <Array> of <Component> of Data.Work.

11. Set the **Expression** to workArray.work.

12. Click on the pencil icon in **Loop Data Output** and create an argument called **loopDataOutput** of type <Array> of <Component> of Data.Work.

13. Set **Expression** to workArray.work.

Inter-process Communication in Practice

Your properties should look similar to the following screenshot:

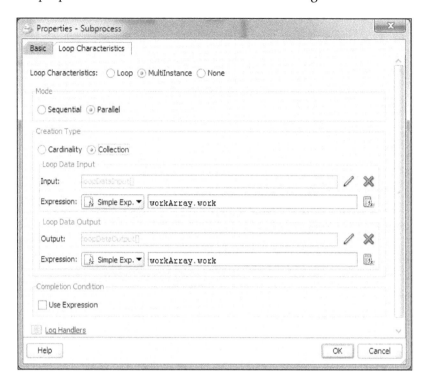

Let's review what we have just done here. We have configured the embedded sub-process to be a **multi-instance sub-process**. BPM creates one instance of the sub-process for each item in the collection Data.work. The item is passed into the instance and copied back to the same place in the collection in the parent instance when the sub-process is complete. This means that any changes made in the sub-process are reflected in the correct item of the collection.

Now, we need to define a **scoped conversation** inside the embedded sub-process. You may recall that we need to do this in the **Structure** pane:

1. Expand **Activities | Activities | Subprocess | Conversations** as shown in the screenshot that follows.

2. Right-click on **Conversations** and create a new conversation named **conversation1**.

3. Set **Type** to **Process Call** and select **Process:** as **Called**:

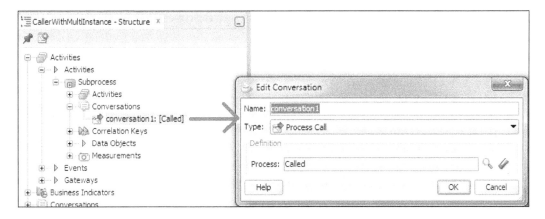

We also need a **scoped correlation key** inside the embedded sub-process:

4. In the **Structure** pane, expand out the **Activities** tree until you find **Correlation Keys**.

5. Right-click on **Correlation Keys** and select **New**. Make sure you choose the one inside the **Subprocess** activity, not the one at the process (top-level) scope.

6. Name the new correlation key as **scoped_key_number** and add the `number` property to it.

7. Now, let's configure the send and receive tasks, as we did in the previous practice activity.

8. Open the **Implementation** tab for **SendTask**.

9. Set **Message Exchange Type** to **Process Call**.

10. Set **Conversation** to **Advanced**—we will be using the **advanced** (non-default) **conversation** in this practice activity.

11. Set **Conversation:** as **conversation1** and **Target Node:** as **ReceiveTask**.

12. Open **Data Associations**. This practice requires a slightly more complicated mapping. On the left-hand side, expand **Subprocess | Predefined Variables** and find **inputDataItem**. Map this to `argument1` on the right-hand side of the screen.

13. Click on **Correlations | Switch to Advanced Mode**. Click on the add icon and select **scoped_key_number** and **Initiates**. Map the `number` property to `argument1.number`.

Your **Properties - SendTask** and **Data Associations** should look similar to the following screenshot:

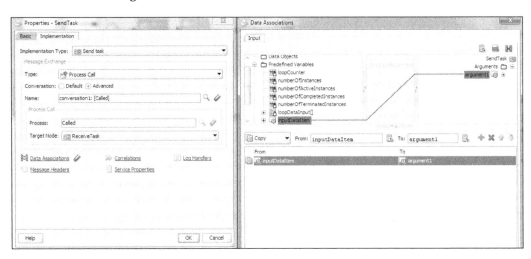

14. Open the **Implementation** tab for **ReceiveTask**. Set **Message Exchange Type** to **Process Call**.

15. Set **Conversation** to **Advanced**. Set **Conversation:** as **conversation1** and **Target Node:** as **SendTask**.

16. Open **Data Associations**. On the right-hand side, expand **Subprocess | Predefined Variables**, and find **outputDataItem**. Map `output1` on the left-hand side of the screen to `outputDataItem`.

17. Click on **Correlations | Switch to Advanced Mode**. Click on the add icon and select **scoped_key_number** but do not check **Initiates** this time. Map the `number` property to `output1.number`.

Now, you can deploy the updated project and start a test instance of `CallerWithMultiInstance`. In the test screen, set the size of the input array (`work`) by entering a value in the array size box and hitting the little refresh icon beside it. (See the red arrow in the following screenshot.)

Then enter some test data as shown in the following screenshot and run the instance:

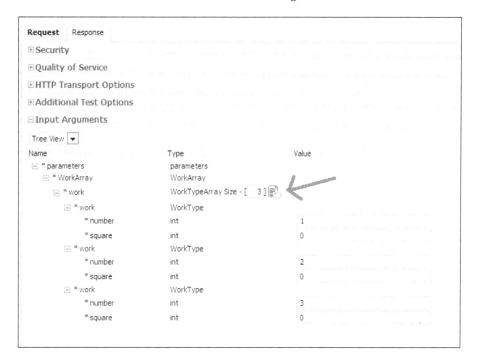

Take a look at the instance in Enterprise Manager. You will see that three instances of the Called process are started (in this case)—one for each item in the input collection (work). When the process instance has completed, you can take a look at the data after the loop to verify that the correct answer got back to each instance of the sub-process.

This practice activity has allowed us to explore the use of a scoped conversation and how correlation works with an advanced conversation (not the default conversation). We saw how to define the scoped conversation inside an embedded sub-process.

Communicating between processes using signals

In this practice activity, we will explore how to use **signals** to create **publish/ subscribe** style communication between process instances, as illustrated in the following diagram. You may recall that when using signals, the sending process does not know which (if any) other processes will receive the signal.

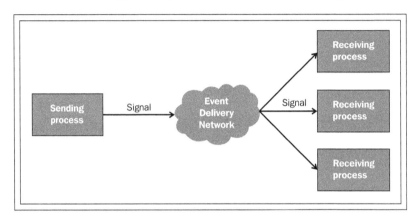

1. Create a new BPM Application in JDeveloper. Name both the application and the project as `Practice3`. Choose the option to create an emty composite.

    Let's start by defining an event. First, we will need a data type definition for the event. We will place this in an XSD file:

2. Create a new XSD file as `myEvent.xsd`. You may need to change to the **All Technologies** tab in **New Gallery** and choose **XML** on the left-hand side and **XML Schema** on the right-hand side of the screen.

3. Right-click on **exampleElement** and add **sequence** inside it. Then, right-click on **sequence** and add an **element** inside that.

4. Right-click on **element** and set its **type** to **xsd:string**. Your XSD should look similar to the following screenshot:

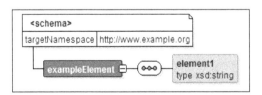

    Obviously, in a real project you would define a more detailed and meaningful structure for your events:

5. Create an event by clicking on the lightning icon in composite (see the red arrow in the diagram that follows).

6. Click on the green plus icon to add an event called **EventDefinition1** and for **Type** choose `exampleElement` that you just defined:

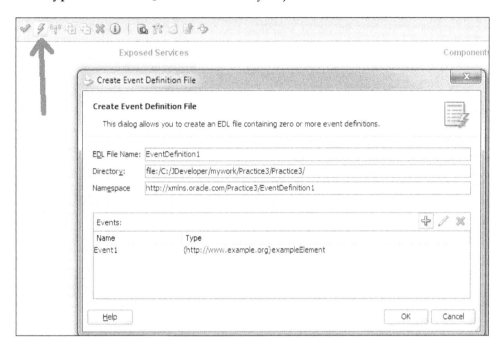

Now, let's create the process that will send the event.

7. Create a new **Process** named **Sender** and choose the **Asynchronous Service** type.

8. Add a throw signal event to this process between the **Start** and **End** nodes.

    Your process should look similar to the following screenshot:

9. Open the **Implementation** tab for **ThrowEvent**. Choose the event that you just defined as **Event1**. Click on **Data Associations** and drop a function on `element1` under `payload` on the right-hand side of the screen.

10. Set this to some arbitrary text such as **"hello"**.

11. Your **Properties - ThrowEvent** and **Data Associations** should look similar to the following screenshot:

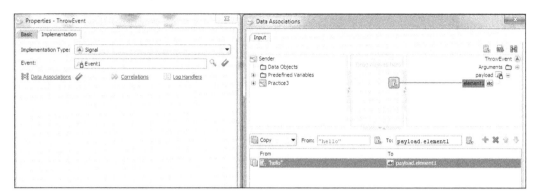

Next, let's create a process to receive the signal:

12. Create another **Process** called **Receiver**. Choose the **Asynchronous Service** type.

13. Right-click on the **Start** node and change its **Trigger Type** to **Signal**. Right-click on the **End** node and change its **Trigger Type** to **None**.

14. Add **Activity** between the **Start** and **End** nodes. Right-click on it and select **Mark Node as Draft**.

Your process should look similar to the following screenshot:

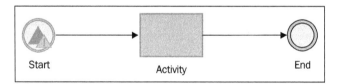

We don't actually care what this process does with the event in this practice activity, just that it gets the signal so that we can mark the activity as **draft**. This tells BPM that we have not implemented the activity yet.

Let's define a process data object to hold the data from the event:

1. Create a new process data object as **theEvent** with the **Type** set to **<Component>** and **Types.ExampleElement**.

2. Open the **Implementation** tab for the start node. Choose **Event1** and open **Data Associations**. Map payload to theEvent.

Your properties should look similar to the following screenshot:

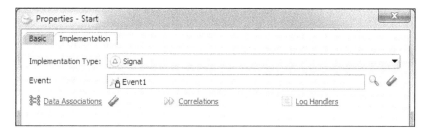

3. Now repeat the steps that you just used to create `Receiver` to create another process called `AnotherReceiver`. Your project will now contain three processes—one that sends a signal and two that will receive it.

Go ahead and deploy your project and run a test instance of the `Sender` process. Use Enterprise Manager to validate that each of the receiver processes has received the signal, as shown in the following screenshot:

In this practice activity, we have seen how to use signals to implement the publish/ subscribe style of communications between processes. If you wish to experiment further, you might like to try sending a signal to or from a different type of component, such as a BPEL process or a Mediator. You might also like to experiment with a more detailed event definition, perhaps make a decision in the receiving process, and take different actions based on the content of the signal.

Using reusable sub-processes

In this practice activity, we want to explore how to use **reusable sub-processes**. You may recall from *Chapter 1, Inter-process Communication,* that a reusable sub-process follows the pattern of starting with a **Start** node with type **None** and ending with an **End** node with type **None**. They are called from a parent process with the **Call** activity.

The `Called` process that we created in the first two practice activities actually follows this pattern; however, we did not use a **Call** activity to invoke it in those practice activities.

You may also recall from *Chapter 1, Inter-process Communication,* that a reusable sub-process does not have access to its parent's **variables** unless they are passed in by the parent as **arguments**. In a reusable sub-process, you define the input and output arguments for the process at the process level, not on the **Start** and **End** nodes.

The **Receive** and **Send** tasks in the `Called` process we saw earlier are not the mechanism used for passing data in and out of reusable processes. So the `Called` process we saw earlier is technically not a reusable sub-process.

Let's create a real reusable sub-process now:

1. Create a new BPM Application in JDeveloper. Name both the application and the project as **Practice4**. Choose the option to create an empty composite.

2. Create a new **Process** called **ReusableProcess** and choose the **Reusable Process** type. Add **Script Task** between the **Start** and **End** nodes.

   Your process should look similar to the following screenshot:

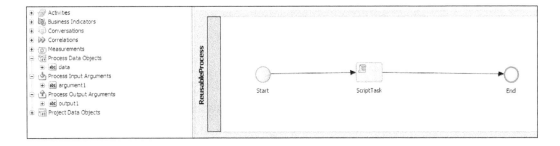

3. Go to the **Structure** pane, as shown on the left-hand side of the previous diagram. Notice that there are two extra options—**Process Input Arguments** and **Process Output Arguments**. This is where we can define the input and output arguments for the reusable sub-process respectively.

4. Create a new process data object called **data** of type `String`. Create a **Process Input Argument** called `argument1` of type `String`. Create a **Process Output Argument** called `output1` of type `String`.

5. Open the **Implementation** tab for the **Start** node and then **Data Associations**. Map `argument1` to `data`.

6. Open the **Implementation** tab for the **End** node and then **Data Associations**. Map `data` to `output1`.

7. Open the **Implementation** tab for **Script Task** and then **Data Associations**. Drag a function and drop it on `data` on the right-hand side of the screen.

8. In the **From:** field, type **data + "hanged in reusable subprocess"** as shown in the following diagram:

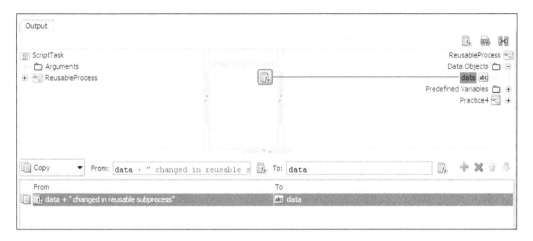

9. Create another **Process** called **ParentProcess** and choose the **Asynchronous Service** type.

10. Add a **Call** activity to this process between its **Start** and **End** nodes. Open the **Implementation** tab for the **Call** activity.

11. Select **ReusableProcess** as the **Process** to call. Open **Data Associations**.

12. Drag a function onto `argument1` and set the **From:** field to **"first"**.

13. Repeat these steps to add a second **Call** activity that calls **ReusabeProcess** and passes in **"second"** as `argument1`.

    Your process should look similar to the following screenshot:

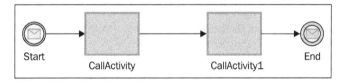

Now deploy your project and run **Instance of ParentProcess** and review the instance in Enterprise Manager. It should look similar to the following screensht:

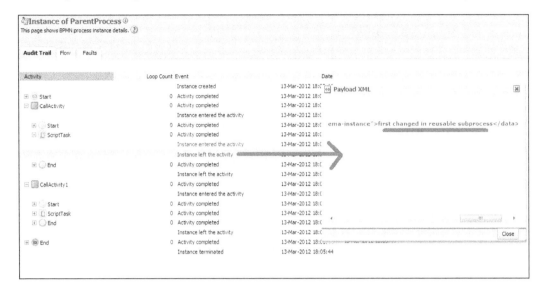

 Let's take a moment to notice an important difference. You can see that the reusable sub-process actually run as part of the parent process's instance. You will not see separate instances for the reusable sub-processes — they share the parent's instance.

You can click on **Instance left the activity** after the `ScriptTask` activities to open the payload at that point. Notice that each time you use the reusable sub-process it has its own set of data — that data which you passed in as arguments. You may recall that a reusable sub-process cannot access the data in its parent process unless it is explicitly passed in as arguments.

Another important characteristic of reusable sub-processes to recall from *Chapter 1, Inter-process Communication,* is that they are not exposed outside of the composite in which they are defined. They can only be called by other BPMN processes — no other type of component (BPEL, Mediator, Spring context, Adapter, and so on) can call them, only BPMN processes.

In this practice activity, we have learned how to create and consume a reusable sub-process, a special type of process that can be used to share logic between processes within a composite. We have also reviewed some of the important differences and limitations of reusable sub-processes.

Summary

In this chapter, we have practiced the skills learned in *Chapter 1, Inter-process Communication*. Specifically, we have looked at how to use correlation with the default conversation to communicate between instances of processes. We have seen that each of the instances of the calling process started a conversation with an instance of the called process, and each reply was sent back to the correct caller.

We explored the use of a scoped conversation and how correlation works with an advanced conversation (not the default conversation). We saw how to define the scoped conversation inside an embedded sub-process.

We also saw how to create and use a reusable sub-process and reviewed some important characteristics and limitations of reusable sub-processes.

The embedded sub-process is a very useful construct for dealing with collections of data. In the next chapter, we will move on to explore how to work with arrays and collections of data in more detail.

3
Working with Arrays

It is often necessary to handle a set of data in a process, which is represented as an array. Some examples of when this may occur include:

- When you retrieve a set of records from a database
- When you are processing a group of related items, for example, order lines in an order

Handling arrays can provide a challenge to the new developer who sometimes finds that the methods they have learned for other data types do not seem to work with arrays. In this chapter, we will present the basic theory on how to deal with arrays, specifically the following:

- Creating an empty array (with no elements)
- Creating an array (with some empty elements)
- Creating an initialized array (with data in it)
- Getting an element of an array
- Setting up an element of an array,
- Appending an element to an array
- Joining two arrays
- Removing an element from an array
- Iterating over an array using an embedded sub-process

We will also put this theory into practice by building a number of example processes to understand how to apply the theory.

BPMN uses one-based, not zero-based arrays. So, `someArray[1]` will give you the first element in the array. You do not use `someArray[0]` to get the first element as you would in languages like C or Java.

Data Associations

In this chapter, we will be referring to some features of the Data Association editor that you should be familiar with. You might like to take a moment before you begin this chapter to refresh your memory.

Notice the two highlighted areas in the screenshot that follows. The one on the left-hand side of the screenshot is called **operation**. There are a number of operations available. You choose an operation for each data mapping (each line in the bottom pane of the editor):

- **Copy**: This operation allows you to copy from one object to another and should be used with objects that are not arrays.

- **Copy List**: This operation allows you to copy from one group of objects (called a "node set") to another and should be used with arrays.

- **Append**: This operation allows you to append an individual object or a group of objects to another and can be used with both arrays and other objects.

- **Insert After**: This operation allows you to insert an object into a group of objects, after the specified object. It should have an object that is not an array on the left and an array on the right.

- **Insert Before**: This operation is similar to Insert After but allows you to insert an object into a group of objects before the specified object.

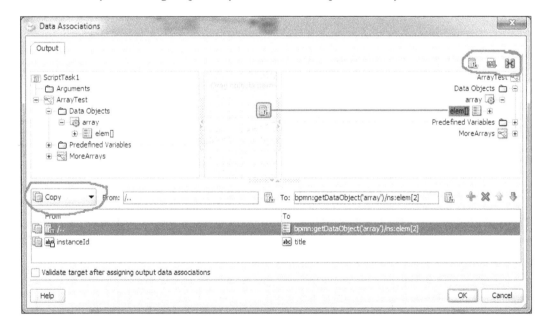

In the top-right corner, there is a group of three icons highlighted. It is important to understand what these are for:

- **Expression**: This is the leftmost icon and it looks like a calculator. This allows you to enter an expression as the source of data mapping; this can be a simple expression or an XPath expression.

- **XML Literal**: This is the center icon. It allows you to use an XML literal (document) as the source of data mapping.

- **XSLT**: This is the rightmost icon. It allows you to execute an XSLT transformation to perform data mapping.

Creating an empty array

Some common scenarios when you may want to create an empty array are when you want to:

- Collect several pieces of data in an array over time for later processing, for example, you may wish to collect the outcome of several human tasks

- Store the output of an **XPath function** that returns a **node set**

While you can create an empty array, you cannot actually use it for anything meaningful until you put some elements into it.

You can create an empty array by using the **Copy** action and **XML Literal** in the Data Association editor. This is shown in the following screenshot, which uses a **Copy** operation with **XML Literal** to create an empty array. It then immediately uses an **Append** operation to store the output of an XPath function into that array.

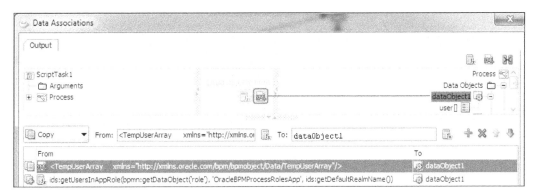

Creating an empty array before storing data in it using the **Append** operation ensures that there will not be a superfluous initial element in the array with no associated value.

Let's practice creating an empty array now. We will use the scenario of creating an array to store outcomes from various user tasks. Our array will hold two values — user and outcome.

1. In JDeveloper, create a new **BPM Application** and name it as **PracticeArrays**.

2. Name the **BPM Project** as **PracticeArrays**.

3. Select the option to create a composite with a BPMN process.

4. Name the **BPMN Process** as Array1.

We are going to create some data types now. We will reuse these same data types in a number of practice exercises in this chapter. We are going to define them in an XSD and then catalog them in BPM Business Catalog. It is a good idea to always define your types this way so that they will be visible to other components, such as business rules for example. If you do not define your data types in XSDs, they will be visible just within BPMN processes.

5. Create a new XML Schema named myArrayTypes.xsd by selecting **New** from the **File** menu. Choose the **All Technologies** tab, then **XML** on the left-hand side and **XML Schema** on the right-hand side of the screen. Make sure you put this new file in your project's XSD directory.

Downloading the example code

You can download the example code files for all Packt books you have purchased from your account at http://www.PacktPub.com. If you purchased this book elsewhere, you can visit http://www.PacktPub.com/support and register to have the files e-mailed directly to you.

6. Switch to the source editor (using the **Source** tab at the bottom of the editor) and paste the following content into the file. You can copy this content from the myArrayTypes.xsd file in the code bundle for this chapter.

```xml
<?xml version="1.0" encoding="UTF-8" ?>
<xsd:schema xmlns:xsd="http://www.w3.org/2001/XMLSchema"
  xmlns:ns="http://www.example.org"
  targetNamespace="http://www.example.org"
  elementFormDefault="qualified">
  <xsd:complexType name="TElement">
    <xsd:sequence>
      <xsd:element name="user" type="xsd:string"/>
      <xsd:element name="outcome" type="xsd:string"/>
    </xsd:sequence>
  </xsd:complexType>
```

```
<xsd:element name="elem" type="ns:TElement">
</xsd:element>
<xsd:element name="array">
  <xsd:complexType>
    <xsd:sequence>
      <xsd:element name="elem" type="ns:TElement"
       maxOccurs="unbounded"/>
    </xsd:sequence>
  </xsd:complexType>
</xsd:element>
</xsd:schema>
```

7. Open the **BPM Project Navigator** and navigate to **Business Catalog**.

8. Right-click on **Business Catalog** and create a new **Module** named **Data**.

9. Right-click on your new **Data** module and create a **Business Object** called **Array** and choose the **Based on External Schema** option. Select the `Array` type that we just defined in the XSD, as shown in the following screenshot:

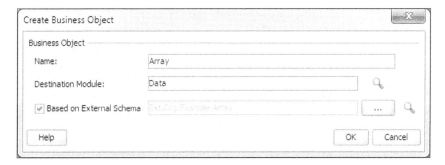

10. Create another **Business Object** named **Elem** using the `Elem` type we defined in the XSD.

11. Create a **Process Data Object** named **myArray** using the `Array` type. In the Business Object you just cataloged, right-click on **Process Data Object** in the **Structure** pane and select **New**:

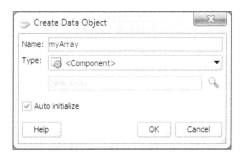

me
12. Add a **Script** activity to your process between the **Start** and **End** activities. Name it **CreateEmptyArray**. Your process should look similar to the following screenshot:

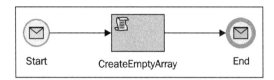

13. Open the **Implementation** tab in **Properties** for `CreateEmptyArray` and click on **Data Associations**.

14. Drag **XML Literal** on to `myArray` on the right-hand side of the screen. Paste the following XML into **XML Literal**. You can copy this content from the `EmptyArray.xml` file in the code bundle for this chapter.

```
<exam:array xmlns:exam="http://www.example.org">
</exam:array>
```

Your **Data Associations** should look similar to the following screenshot:

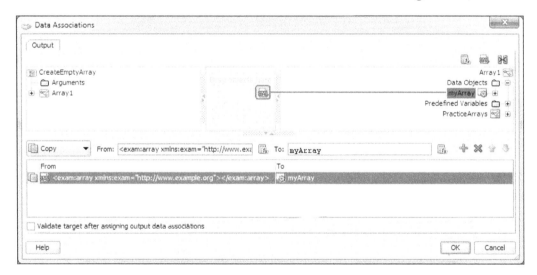

Deploy your project to your BPM Server and run a test instance of the process `Array1`.

15. Open **Flow Trace** for this instance and then look at the payload in the **Instance left the activity** event for `CreateEmptyArray`, that is, after our data associations have been executed. It should look similar to the following screenshot:

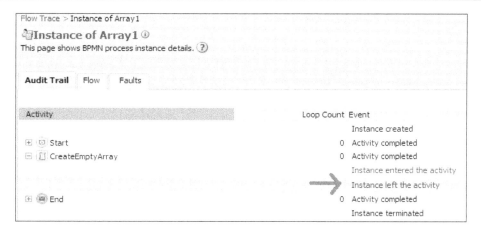

Your payload should resemble this. The part that is highlighted (in bold) is the array we created. Notice that the array has no elements in it—it is an empty array:

```
<auditQueryPayload  auditId="413004"  ciKey="170002">
  <dataState>
    <dataObject  name="myArray"  isBusinessIndicator="false">
      <value> <array xmlns:exam="http://www.example.org"
        xmlns="http://www.example.org"> </array> </value>
    </dataObject>
  </dataState>
</auditQueryPayload>
```

We have created an empty array.

 We will reuse the data types in future practice activities, so you should create new processes in the same project.

Creating an array with some empty elements

To create an array with one or more empty elements in it, you first create an empty array (as shown in the preceding section), and then you append the number of empty elements that you need. If you need more than one, then you could use a loop.

You can append the empty element using the **Append** operation in the Data Association editor, as we saw in the previous example. To get an empty element to append, you just need to define a data object based on the business object of the type you need, but don't put any data in it.

Let's update our `Array1` process to add some empty elements to our array:

1. Add a **Subprocess** activity to your process after `CreateEmptyArray`. Open the **Loop Characteristics** tab in **Properties** and choose **Loop**. Set the **Loop Condition** to **loopCounter <= 5**. This `loopCounter` we referred to is a predefined variable that will automatically be incremented each time the loop is executed:

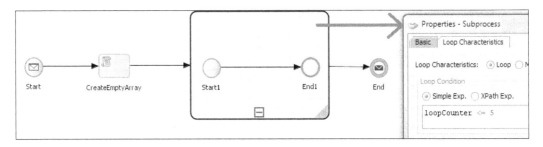

2. Let's create the new empty data object that we will use to populate the array. In the **Structure** view, open the **Activities** tree and navigate to your **Subprocess** activity's **Data Objects** and right-click to create a new one. Name it as **innerElem** and set **Type** to **Data.Elem**, as shown in the following screenshot:

3. Add a new **Script** activity inside your **Subprocess** and name it as **AddEmptyElement**, as shown in the following screenshot:

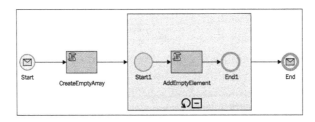

4. Open the **Implementation** tab for **AddEmptyElement** and click on **Data Associations**.

5. Drag **XPath Function** and drop it on **myArray** as indicated by the red arrow in the following screenshot:

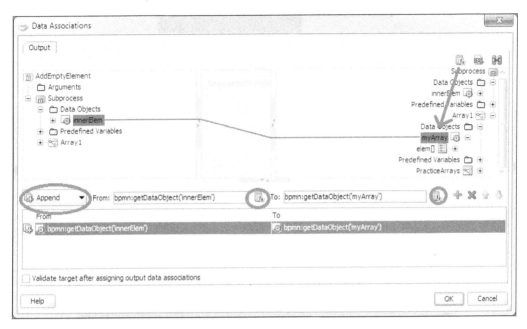

6. Change the mode to **Append** as indicated by the red highlighted drop-down on the left-hand side of the preceding screenshot.

7. Click on **XPath function** icons for the **From** value, as shown by the small red circles in the preceding screenshot, and ensure that the mode is set to **XPath Exp.** and the value is **bpmn:getDataObject('innerElem').**

8. Repeat the last step to ensure the **To** value is set to **XPath Exp.** with the value set as **bpmn:getDataObject('myArray').**

9. Your **Data Associations** should look the same as the preceding screenshot.

10. Now go ahead and deploy your updated process and run a test instance. You may wish to choose a new **revision number** during the deployment so that you can keep both versions of this process deployed.

11. Open **Flow Trace** for the instance and take a look at the payload in the **Instance left the activity** event after `AddEmptyElement` in the last iteration of the loop, as highlighted in the following screenshot:

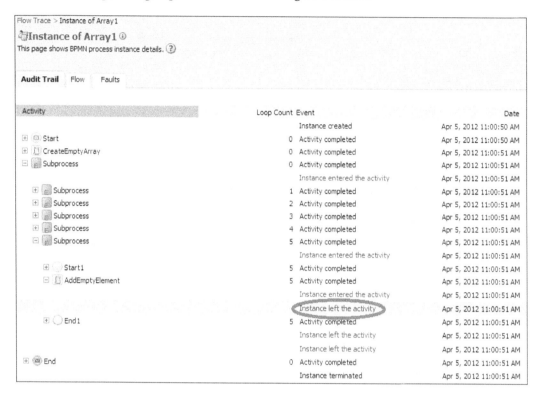

Here is the contents of the payload—note that we have added line breaks to make it easier to read:

```
<array xmlns:exam="http://www.example.org"
  xmlns="http://www.example.org">
  <elem><user/><outcome/></elem>
  <elem><user/><outcome/></elem>
  <elem><user/><outcome/></elem>
  <elem><user/><outcome/></elem>
  <elem><user/><outcome/></elem>
</array>
```

We have created an array with five empty elements in it.

Creating an initialized array

You can create an initialized array using a **Copy** operation with **XML Literal** as the source and a process data object of the array type as the destination. Here is an example of **XML Literal** that is suitable for initializing an array. You can find this content in the file `initializedArray.xml` in the code bundle for this chapter.

```
<exam:array xmlns:exam="http://www.example.org">
  <exam:elem>
    <exam:user>user1</exam:user>
    <exam:outcome>APPROVE</exam:outcome>
  </exam:elem>
  <exam:elem>
    <exam:user>user2</exam:user>
    <exam:outcome>REJECT</exam:outcome>
  </exam:elem>
</exam:array>
```

Let's try this now.

1. Add a new **Process** to your project. Name it as **Array2**.

2. Define a process data object named **myArray** of type `Data.Array`.

3. Add a **Script** activity to the process. Name it **InitializeArray**.

4. Open the **Implementation** tab for **InitializeArray** and click on **Data Associations**.

5. Drag **XML Literal** on to **myArray** and copy the preceding example into it.

6. Deploy your process and run a test instance. Choose a new revision number during the deployment so that you do not overwrite your previous practice exercises.

7. Open **Flow Trace** for your test instance and take a look at the payload in the **Instance left the activity** event for `InitializeArray` step.

Your payload should look like the following example—note that we have reformatted this example to make it easier to read:

```
<array xmlns:exam="http://www.example.org"
  xmlns="http://www.example.org">
  <exam:elem>
    <exam:user>user1</exam:user>
    <exam:outcome>APPROVE</exam:outcome>
  </exam:elem>
```

```
    <exam:elem>
      <exam:user>user2</exam:user>
      <exam:outcome>REJECT</exam:outcome>
    </exam:elem>
  </array>
```

We have created an array with initialized elements.

Getting elements from arrays

To get an element in an array, refer to it using its index in brackets after the name of the array, for example, SomeBusinessObject.MyArray[2] refers to the second element in MyArray.

You can use this syntax in the source of an operation in the Data Association editor or in any other place where you can write an expression, for example, in a log handler, in the properties for a loop, or in a gateway condition (a decision point in a process).

Setting elements in arrays

You can set an element in an array using a **Copy** operation in the Data Association editor. The target should be the name of the array with the element index in brackets, for example, SomeBusinessObject.MyArray[2].

The source can be an **XML Literal**, the output of an XPath function that returns an object of the correct type, or a data object (variable) of the correct type.

Appending elements to arrays

To append new items to an array, you use the **Append** operation in the Data Association editor. The target should be the array itself, as opposed to the last element in the array.

The source can be **XML Literal**, the output of an XPath function that returns an object of the correct type, or a data object (variable) of the correct type.

This technique can be used regardless of whether the target array is empty or not.

We have already used this technique in the practice exercise for *Creating an initialized array* earlier in this chapter.

Joining two arrays

To join two arrays, you can just append each element of the second array to the end of the first array like we did in the previous examples. You could do this by using the **Append** operation in the Data Association editor inside a loop that iterates over the elements in the second array. We will cover iterating over arrays shortly.

Removing elements from arrays

BPM does not provide any specific mechanism to remove an element from an array, so the approach that you should use is to copy the array into a new array, omitting those elements that you want to remove. If the element you want to remove is the first or last element in the array, this can be done with a single operation, copying all of the other elements. Otherwise, you could copy the element(s) before the one you wish to remove and then append the elements after it to the new array.

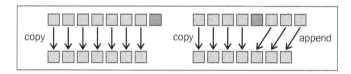

Copying elements can be done using the process described above to create an initialized array. Appending the remaining elements can be done using the procedure described above for joining two arrays.

Iterating over arrays with a multi-instance embedded sub-process

The multi-instance embedded sub-process gives you an advanced mechanism to iterate over arrays. In particular, it allows you to execute the iterations in parallel. It provides more advanced mechanisms to specify what you want to iterate over, and it provides a "short circuit" mechanism to break out of the loop early.

Let's review the main characteristics of the multi-instance embedded sub-process.

Cardinality or collection

A multi-instance embedded sub-process can use **cardinality** or **collection** to define the number of iterations the loop will execute:

- When you choose cardinality, you provide an expression that evaluates to a number. This can be a simple expression or an XPath expression. This number specifies how many times the loop body will execute.

- When you choose to use a collection, you specify the collection you are interested in and the loop body will be executed once for each element in the array.

These two choices are quite similar but there is a subtle difference. Consider the two following short code samples, which are written in Java but are fairly similar to C# and other common languages that you may be familiar with.

```
Object[] data = something();
for (int i = 0; i < data.length; i++) {
  doSomethingTo(data[i]);
}
```

This example uses cardinality. Notice that there is a local variable i that tells you which element of the array/collection you are currently visiting. This creates the opportunity to manipulate this variable to move backwards and forward through the collection if you wanted to do so.

```
for (object x : data) {
  doSomethingTo(x);
}
```

This example uses a collection; each item in the collection is visited exactly once, and when you are inside the logic you have no way of knowing the cardinality/number of the item you are dealing with, whether it is the first, second, or third item in the collection. This style of iteration is particularly useful when you are changing the collection as you iterate over it, for example, by adding items to or removing items from the collection.

For the purposes of comparison, the normal embedded sub-process with **Type** set to **Loop** (as opposed to **Multi-Instance**) can behave just like a Java while or do ... while loop, as shown in the following two code examples.

```
while (someCondition) {
  doSomething();
}
```

```
do {
  doSomething();
} while (someCondition);
```

The first example is the behavior when the loop condition is set to evaluate before the loop body, and the second example when it is set to evaluate after.

Sequential or parallel

You can choose to have the multiple instances that are created – one for each execution of the loop body – to run one after the other (sequentially) or in parallel. If you choose to run them in parallel, each one will run in its own thread, independently of the others. The multi-instance embedded sub-process will complete when all of the instances have completed unless something happens to force execution to end early. Examples of things that could cause an early end are an interrupting boundary event, an interrupting event sub-process, a fault that causes the process instance to be suspended or aborted, or reaching a **completion condition** if one is specified. Completion conditions will be discussed in the next section.

You can nest other embedded sub-processes (multi-instance or otherwise) inside a multi-instance embedded sub-process. If you do this, you can mix and match between parallel and sequential. For example, you can have the outer sub-process instances run in parallel and the inner sub-process instances run sequentially.

Using a completion condition

You have the option of also specifying a completion condition. If this condition evaluates to `true` at any time during the execution of the multi-instance embedded sub-process, then the execution of all of the sub-process instances will end immediately, the embedded sub-process will complete, and execution will continue with the next activity in the parent process.

Completion conditions are useful when you are searching for items in a collection and you are not sure if they are there, or where in the collection they are. Once you have found them, there is no need to continue searching the rest of the collection.

Scope

Remember that just like normal embedded sub-processes, the multi-instance variety also allows you to add boundary events to created scoped exception handling. You can also define a scoped conversation inside the embedded sub-process. This is particularly useful – practically essential – if you want to call the same process or service from every instance of the embedded sub-process.

Practice: Iterating over an array using an embedded sub-process

Let's practice this now by iterating over one of the arrays we created earlier:

1. Return to your `Array2` process, which should look similar to the following diagram:

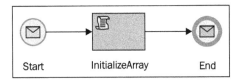

2. Add a **Subprocess** activity after **InitializeArray**.

3. Add a **Script** activity to **Subprocess** and name it as **DoSomething**. Since we don't actually care what we do with data for the purposes of this activity, select the **Is Draft** option on the **Basic** tab in **Properties** for **DoSomething**.

   Your process should now look similar to the following diagram:

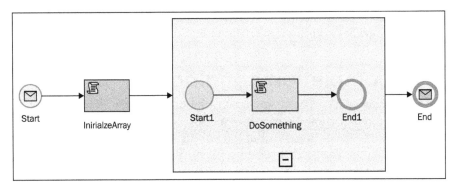

4. Now, let's set up the iteration. Open the **Loop Characteristics** tab in **Properties** for **Subprocess**.

5. Set **Loop Characteristics** to **MultiInstance**.

6. Set **Mode** to **Sequential**.

7. Set **Creation Type** to **Collection**.

8. Click on the pencil icon to define **Loop Data Input**. In the dialog box, set **Type** to **<Array>**, **Element Type** to **<Component>**, and choose **Data.Elem** as **Type**, as shown in the following diagram:

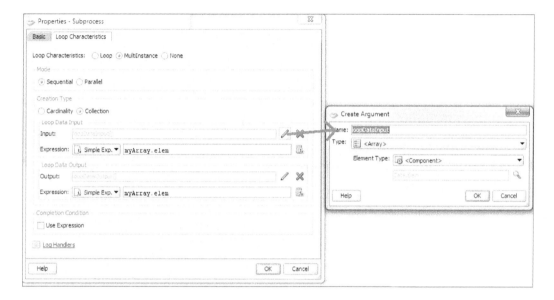

9. Repeat the previous step to define **Loop Data Output** using the same values.

10. Deploy your process and run a test instance. Remember to choose a new revision number during deployment if you want to keep your previous work.

Your **Flow Trace** should show two iterations of the loop, as we see in the following screenshot:

You might like to try updating the data inside the loop to validate for yourself that myArray comes out of **Subprocess** with all of the updates intact. This works for both parallel and sequential executions of multi-instance embedded sub-processes.

Summary

In this chapter, we have explored how to create, manipulate, and iterate over arrays. We have also put this new knowledge to use by building some practical example processes. In these activities, we have seen how to use various features of the Data Association editor, including XML Literals and XPath Expressions to refer to arrays and array data.

In the next chapter, we will start to explore how we handle exceptions in BPM.

4
Handling Exceptions

Exception is a term we use to describe an event that occurs in the execution of a business process that is not normal. It does not imply that the event was unexpected, but rather that the event would not usually occur when the business process was executed under normal circumstances. In fact, part of designing a high quality process is ensuring that you anticipate exceptions that may occur and model exception handling logic into your process definition.

There are different kinds of exceptions that can occur in a business process. Broadly, we categorize these into two groups:

- **Business exceptions**: These are exceptional circumstances that occur from a business point of view. For example, in an ordering process the unavailability of inventory to fulfill an order could be considered a business exception. With good business engagement and modeling practices, it is possible to understand most, if not all, possible business exceptions for a given business process and include appropriate handling logic in your process definition.

- **System exceptions**: These are failures that occur in the IT environment. For example, the unavailability of the product database when attempting to retrieve information about a product would be considered a system exception. It tends to be difficult to predict when these kinds of failures might occur, although it is reasonably straightforward to understand what kinds of failures could possibly occur. System exceptions might be handled with a different approach, using the "Fault Management Framework", rather than building logic into your process definitions to handle them.

Importantly, exceptions should not be used to control the "normal" flow of execution in the business process. This is similar to the principle of not using exceptions to control flow in a Java program as an example. Exceptions should be caught and handled if possible. Execution of the process should then be allowed to continue if possible, or the process instance should be terminated if it is not possible for execution to continue.

Mechanisms for catching exceptions in BPMN

BPMN provides two mechanisms for catching exceptions — the **boundary event** and the **event sub-process**. The semantics of these two mechanisms are quite different, and they should be used in different circumstances.

Boundary events

The **boundary event** can be attached to an **activity** or to an **embedded sub-process**. It provides a mechanism to capture an event, message, or signal if it occurs while the activity or sub-process that the boundary event is attached to is being executed. Boundary events can be defined as **interrupting** or **non-interrupting**.

When an event is caught by an interrupting boundary event, the task or sub-process execution is suspended, and execution continues with the first task attached to the default flow from the boundary event. When an event is caught by a non-interrupting boundary event, then the task or sub-process execution continues and a new thread of execution starts from the activity after the boundary event.

Interrupting boundary events are shown with a solid border. Non-interrupting boundary events are shown with a dotted border, similar to the ones attached to the Approve Order activity in the following diagram:

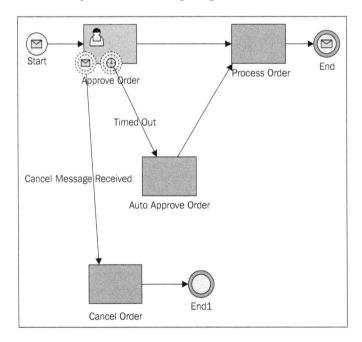

There are five types of events that you can "catch" on a boundary:

- **Error**: This boundary event lets you catch a system or business exception that causes an error (fault) to be created.
- **Message**: This boundary event lets you respond to the receipt of a message from another process.
- **Signal**: This boundary event lets you catch a signal from another process.
- **Timer**: This boundary event allows you to specify a period of time and is useful for creating an "expiry" time on a task or sub-process.
- **None**: This boundary event has no actual purpose at runtime. It is used when you know that you need to include a boundary event in the model, but you are not ready to define all of the details yet, for example, you may know that it will be a message boundary event, but the message type is not defined yet.

It is also possible to attach several boundary events to a single task or sub-process, with different exception handling logic attached to each one. They can share some or all of their logic if desired.

Notice that you are able to return to the main flow of the process after you have handled the exception. If the boundary event was interrupting, you can only return to the main flow at a point that the interrupted activity or sub-process could have taken the process after it completed its normal execution.

Note also that the boundary events are only caught while the task they are attached to is being executed. If an instance of the process shown in the preceding diagram had already moved past the `Approve Order` task to the `Process Order` task, and then received a `Cancel` message, the boundary event that catches cancel messages would no longer be active, so the message would be ignored.

Event sub-processes

The second mechanism for handling exceptions is the **event sub-process**. This is a special type of sub-process that is invoked whenever a particular event occurs, no matter where it occurs in the process. These are not specific to a particular task or sub-process like boundary events are. This means they provide a mechanism to have a single set of exception handling logic that will handle a particular exception no matter when, or where, in the process it occurs.

Here is an example of an event sub-process:

Notice that the event sub-process (that's it at the bottom) is not attached to any particular task in the main process. It is triggered by the receipt of a Cancel message in this case, but they can also be triggered by the same range of events as a boundary event — message, signal, error, timer, and none.

Notice that you cannot return to the main process from the event sub-process if it is an interrupting event sub-process. However, if you define the event sub-process as non-interrupting, the main process flow will continue while the event sub-process runs in a parallel thread.

When you define an interrupting event sub-process, if the event sub-process is triggered the main flow of the process will stop, then the event sub-process will run, and the process instance will end. No further tasks in the main flow will be carried out.

An interesting use of non-interrupting event sub-processes is to create a "query" mechanism — a way to ask a process instance a question, like for example, the value of one of its variables. This is possible since the event sub-process has access to the process variables. Note though that this approach works only during the life of the instance — when the instance is complete, you can no longer send it a message.

Exception propagation with sub-processes and peer processes

It is important to understand how exceptions behave when you are using sub-processes and peer processes. In some cases, exceptions that occur in a `Called` process are propagated to the `Calling` process, and in other cases they are not.

Exception propagation with embedded sub-processes

Embedded sub-processes are executed as part of the process that contains them. This means that any exception that occurs in an embedded sub-process will be propagated to the next scope up if it is not caught and handled in that embedded sub-process, for example by a boundary event. This is perhaps best understood with an example. Consider the process illustrated in the following diagram:

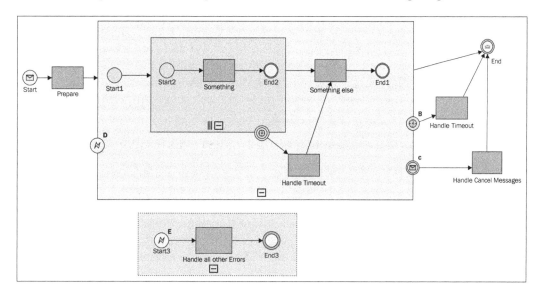

This process contains two embedded sub-processes, one inside the other. It also contains an event sub-process. Let us consider what would happen if an exception occurred in the `Something` activity in the inner sub-process.

The inner sub-process has only one boundary event, which is marked with a red A. It is an interrupting timer boundary event. These are used to set a timeout on the scope they are attached to. In this case, this event would only fire if the time specified were exceeded. If that occurred, control would pass to the `Handle Timeout` activity and then `Something else`. As this is an interrupting boundary event, all of the parallel instances of the inner sub-process would end. So we see that this does not handle our exception, so it is passed to the next scope out, the outer sub-process.

The outer sub-process has three boundary events, let us consider each one in turn:

- The interrupting timer boundary event (B) would catch a timeout, end all instances of the outer sub-process, and pass control to `Handle Timeout` then `End`. This will not handle our exception.

- The interrupting message boundary event (C) would catch a particular message, a `Cancel` message in this example. If such a message arrived while the outer sub-process was executing, all instances of the outer sub-process would end and control would pass to `Handle Cancel Message` and then `End`. This will not handle out exception either.

- The interrupting error boundary event (D) would catch a particular kind of error—a business exception or a system exception. If that particular error occurs, all instances of the outer sub-process end and control passes back to `Prepare`, after which the whole sub-process will be tried again. Let's assume that the exception that occurred is not caught by this boundary event. Therefore, it will be passed up to the next scope out, which is the process itself.

There are three ways that an exception can be handled at the process level:

- If there is an event sub-process that catches the particular type of exception that we have, be it a business or system exception, then control will pass to that event sub-process. It will run in parallel to the main process if it is a non-interrupting event sub-process, or the main process will end if it is an interrupting event sub-process. It is possible to configure an event sub process to catch all possible system and business exceptions, which is what we have done in this example. So in this case, the interrupting event sub-process (E) would catch our exception, which came from the `Something` activity in the inner sub-process, stop the whole process, and pass control to the `Handle all other Errors` activity. Once this is complete, the process instance will end.

- If there is a fault policy attached to the process that handles the type of exception that we have, it will be used to determine what should be done to handle the exception. We will cover fault policies later in this chapter.

- If we get to this point, then there is basically no error handling logic anywhere in our process. Now the exception will be thrown to the next scope out, which is the BPMN engine. The engine will then decide what to do with it. Based on its configuration, it may decide to retry the process instance, or it may place it in a failed state. This could be a recoverable or non-recoverable state. If it is a recoverable state, the engine will try to recover it the next time the recovery job runs (once a day). If it is non-recoverable, the exception will be passed to the next scope out—you! The exception will be reported to you in the audit trail of the process instance and it will be up to you to decide what to do about it.

Note that it could be possible that both the error boundary event (D) and the event sub-process (E) were capable of catching the exception. Exceptions will always be caught by the closest handler first, so the error boundary event (D) would get the exception in that case. Boundary events are evaluated before event sub-processes.

Exception propagation with sub-processes invoked with a call activity

When you invoke a sub-process using a call activity, any system exceptions that occur in the sub-process will propagate to the calling process. You can catch these exceptions with either a boundary event or an event sub-process.

You can throw a business exception from a sub-process using the error end event. These exceptions can only be caught by the calling the (parent) process in this case.

Exception propagation with peer processes invoked with a throw event

When you start a peer process using a throw event and an exception occurs in the called process, the exception is **not** automatically propagated to the calling process.

This means that you will need to model into your process(es) some logic to handle the situation when the called process fails.

There are two approaches to achieve this:

- Put the logic in the calling process. If you take this approach you have the opportunity to handle failures in a way that is specific to the calling process. This would typically be achieved by placing the throw and the matching catch into a scope (an embedded sub-process) and attaching a boundary catch timer event to that scope.

- Put the logic in the called process. This allows you to reuse the logic. It is normally handled by throwing an exception from the called process back to the calling process, for example by using a throw event. Typically, you would throw the same type (message, signal) back to the caller.

Exception propagation with peer processes invoked with a send task

When you communicate with a peer process using send and receive tasks, any exceptions in the called process will propagate back to the caller as a (SOAP) fault that you can catch and handle as appropriate in the calling process.

How BPM exceptions affect the SCA composite

There is one important consideration to be aware of: if an exception occurs in a BPMN process, even if the BPMN process handles the exception and finishes running successfully, the status of the composite is marked as faulted.

Summary

In this chapter, we have examined the different kinds of exceptions that can occur in a business process and different ways to handle those exceptions. We also looked at how exceptions are (or are not) propagated in various scenarios. Understanding these topics is essential to defining good exception handling in your processes.

We also introduced the Fault Management Framework, which allows us to externalize the fault handling policies from the processes.

In the next chapter, we will put this theory into practice by building a number of examples to help us to fully appreciate how exception handling works in BPM.

5
Handling Exceptions in Practice

In the previous chapter, we explored the theory of handling exceptions in a variety of circumstances and the mechanisms that BPM provides to let us catch, propagate, and handle exceptions. In this chapter, we will put this new knowledge into practice by exploring some practical examples of exception handling:

- Using boundary events to implement timeouts so that our processes do not wait forever for an answer that will never come
- Using boundary events to implement the "cancel message" use case where we want to stop a process if a second message (the cancel message) is received while it is still working
- Using event sub-processes to implement the cancel message use case, and also to look at how to implement an instance data query mechanism
- Propagating exceptions between peer processes

Using boundary events to implement timeouts

The simplest way to see for yourself how boundary events work is to create a simple process with a human task and a timer boundary event set to a suitable time period, for example, one minute. Then, you can start an instance of the process and ignore the human task for a minute to see the boundary event fire.

Let's create this example now:

1. In JDeveloper, create a new **BPM Application** and call it **BoundaryEvents**.
2. Create new **BPM Project** called **BoundaryEvents**.
3. Create new **Process** called **MyTimerEvent**.
4. Move the **End** node aside to create some more space and add a **User** task and two **Activity** tasks to your process. Name the two **Activity** tasks as **Normal Activity** and **Handle Timeout**.
5. Mark both of the **Activity** tasks as draft.
6. Open the **Events** section of the palette, and from the **Catch Events** group drag a **Timer** event into the process. While you are still dragging it, move it on to the edge of the **User** task. It will "attach" itself to the edge of the task. You will see as you move your mouse it stays "stuck" to the edge of the task.
7. From the **End Events** group, add a **Terminate** event to the process.
8. Now wire up your tasks, as shown in the following diagram:

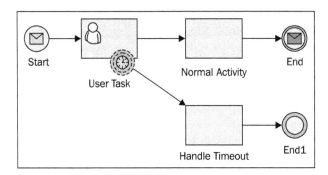

9. Open **Properties - CatchEvent**, and go to the **Implementation** tab. Select **Time Cycle** and set it to one minute, that is, **0 Months 0 Days 0:1:0**, as shown in the following screenshot:

10. Create a human task definition by opening the **Implementation** tab for the **User** task and clicking on the green plus icon. You don't need to define any data or a user interface for this task because you are just going to ignore it after all. So you can just accept all the defaults.

11. Now you can deploy your process and test it. Start an instance of the process and then wait for the timer to fire. Your audit trail should look similar to the following screenshot:

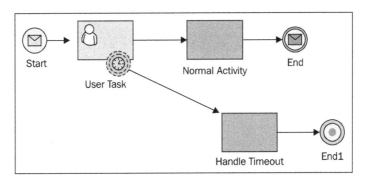

You might like to run another instance of the process and action the human task before the timer fires to validate the process runs as you expect.

Using boundary events to implement the cancel message use case

Putting a boundary event on every task can obviously clutter up your process model very quickly, and often we want to treat a group of activities as atomic — we want them all to happen, or none of them. This leads us naturally to the next level of sophistication in the use of boundary events — grouping activities in a sub-process and attaching boundary events to the sub-process.

Let's take a look at this approach now by building an example around the concept of processing an order, but where the possibility of the order being cancelled exists:

1. Create a new **Process** in your **BoundaryEvents** application and name it **CancelBoundaryEvent**.

 Let's begin by laying out the process, so we can visualize what we are doing. Then, we will go back and define the data we need. In this example, we are going to use correlation so that we can make sure the cancel message goes to the right process instance.

2. Move the **End** node to the side to create some space.

3. Add an embedded sub-process (not an event sub-process) to your process and expand it to make some space inside.

4. Inside the sub-process add **Activity**, then **Timer Catch Event**, then another **Activity**. Name these as **Allocate Stock**, **Wait For Payment**, and **Complete Order** respectively.

5. Open the **Implementation** tab for **Wait For Payment** and set it to **Time Cycle** and one minute, as we did in the previous exercise. This will serve to create a short delay so that we will have time to send the cancel message to the process instance.

6. Now, add **Catch Message Event** to the boundary of the sub-process.

7. Add the **Activity** named **Deallocate Stock** and **Terminate End Event**, and wire up your process as shown in the following diagram:

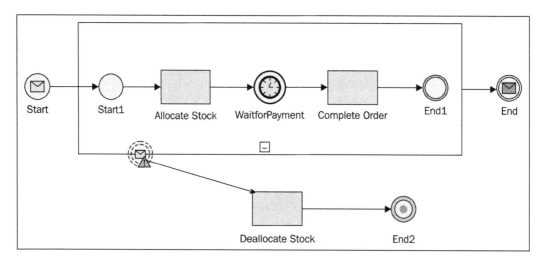

8. Mark all three **Activity** tasks as draft — we don't need them to actually do anything in this example.

Now we have our process laid out and we have an understanding of how it will work. This process will handle an order. First, it will allocate some stock, then it will wait for payment to be processed, and finally it will complete the order. Obviously, a real-life order process would be a little more complicated, for example, the payment may fail and we would need to handle that, but this simple process will do to illustrate the functionality that we are trying to explore here.

The boundary event will fire when a message is sent to cancel the order. This could happen if the customer changes their mind, or wants to add or remove some products to the order, for example. When we get the cancel message, we will de-allocate the stock and then terminate the process instance. Again, this is a somewhat contrived flow designed to demonstrate the boundary event functionality and a real order process would be more sophisticated.

Now, we are going to need some data for this process. We are going to need an order with some unique identifier, and we are going to need two messages: one to start the process and one to cancel the order. We will use correlation to make sure the cancel message goes to the correct instance of the process.

Let's set up our data now:

1. Open **BPM Project Navigator**.
2. Add a new **Module** to **Business Catalog** named **Data**.
3. Add a new **Business Object** called **Order** to your **Data** module.
4. Add three attributes to your **Order**: an Int type named **orderNumber**, a String type named **orderStatus**, and a String type named **otherData**.
5. Return to your process and add a new **Process Data Object** named **Order** of type <Component> and select your new Data.Order business object.
6. Open the **Implementation** tab for the **Start** node and add an argument named **argument1** of type <Component> and select **Data.Order**.
7. Still in the **Implementation** tab for the **Start** node, open **Data Associations** and map argument1 to Order.
8. Still in the **Implementation** tab for the **Start** node, open **Correlations**.
9. Click on the add icon to create a new property. Name it as **theOrderNumber** and set **Type** to **Int**.

10. Check (select) **Initiates** and set **theOrderNumber** to **argument1. orderNumber**, as shown in the following screenshot:

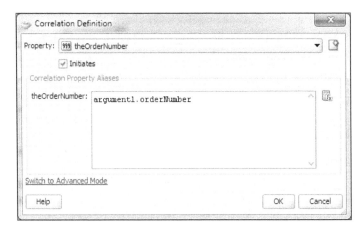

Let's pause for a moment and review what we have just done. We have an order that is made up of an order number, which is our unique identifier for an order, and some other data—we don't care about the other data in this example.

We have set up our process to accept an order as its input when an instance is started. This order is stored in a process data object (variable) inside the instance, and we have configured correlation based on the order number. This means that we can send another message to that process instance using the order number as our correlation key.

Let's set up the cancel message using this approach now:

1. Open the **Implementation** tab for the boundary event.

2. We want this boundary event to stop the main process flow, so check (select) the **Interrupting Event** checkbox.

3. Set **Message Exchange** to **Define Interface**.

4. Add a new argument called **cancelArgument1** of type <Component> and select Data.Order.

5. Open **Correlations**. Select the property **theOrderNumber** and set the value to **cancelArgument1.orderNumber**. Do not select **Initiates**, as shown in the following screenshot:

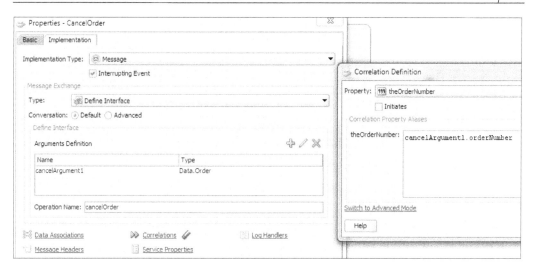

Now let's review again. We have set up the boundary event to receive a message that contains the order number and then to interrupt the main flow of the process, do some clean-up activities, and then terminate the process. For simplicity, we have reused the same business object in this message, but this need not be the case. It is only the order number that we need — as that is the correlation key.

Now, we are ready to see our process in action:

1. Deploy the process to your server and select **New Revision ID** so that you do not overwrite your previous work.

2. Start a few instances of the process with different order numbers, for example, 1, 2, 3, and so on.

3. Send a cancel message for order number 2. Make sure you do this within one minute so that the process has not completed!

 To send the cancel message, select the `cancelOrder` operation from the **Operation** drop-down list after you click on the **Test** button in Enterprise Manager to open the test page.

Validate that the correct order was cancelled and that the other orders were not affected by the cancel message. You may wish to go to the **Instances** tab for your **BoundaryEvents [2.0]** composite so that you can easily see all three process instances at once.

The audit trail for the instance that handled order number 2 should look similar to the following screenshot:

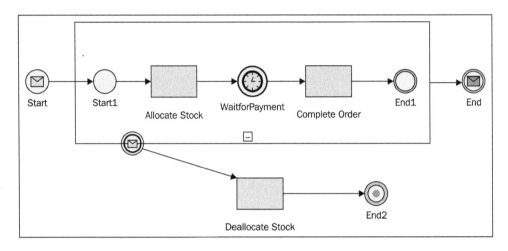

Remember that the cancel message will have no effect after the process instance has moved past the sub-process. You might like to test this for yourself.

Using event sub-processes

In the previous example, we saw how we can use a boundary event to implement the cancel instance use case. We could also use an interrupting event sub-process to implement this use case. After you have completed this example, you might want to go back and implement the cancel order example using an event sub-process.

Another common use case that is implemented using event sub-processes is querying a process instance to retrieve some data from it. This is the use case we will implement in this practical exercise.

First, we will update the CancelBoundaryEvent process from the previous practical exercise so that it updates the orderStatus attribute of the Order process data object as it progresses through the process. Then, we will add an event sub-process that will allow us to query the status of an order.

1. Open the properties for the **Allocate Stock** activity. Remove the draft checkbox, then go to the **Implementation** tab.

2. Change **Implementation Type** to **Script Task**.

3. Open **Data Associations** and drop a function on **orderStatus**. Set the value to **"STOCK ALLOCATED"** (including the quotes), as shown in the following screenshot:

4. Repeat these steps on the **Complete Order** activity so that it sets the **orderStatus** to "PAYMENT PROCESSED".

So we now have two different order statuses as the instance moves through the process. We will be able to see the order status change after the payment is processed—after the one minute delay in the middle of the process. Let's set up an event sub-process now so that we can query the order status.

1. Add **Event Subprocess** into your process—you can just put it down the bottom as it is not going to be connected into the main process.

 To keep things simple, we will reuse the Order business object for the messages that we send and receive from the event sub-process.

2. Open the **Implementation** tab for the **Start** node inside the event sub-process.

3. Set **Message Exchange** to **Define Interface**. Do not check (select) **Interrupting Event**—we do not want this event sub-process to interfere with the main process.

4. Add an argument named **queryArgument1** of type `<Component>` and select `Data.Order`.

5. Open **Correlations**, select the **OrderNumber** property, and set the value to **queryArgument1.orderNumber**. Do not check (select) **Initiates**. This will make sure that we get the correct process instance for the order that we are interested in—just like we did in the previous exercise to make sure the cancel message went to the correct instance.

6. Now open the **Implementation** tab for the **End** node inside the event sub-process.

7. Set **Implementation Type** to **Message**.

8. Set **Message Exchange** to **Define Interface**.

9. Add an argument named **queryResult1** of type `<Component>` and select `Data.Order`.

10. Change the interface to **Synchronous** and in the **Reply To** field, select the name of the **Start** node in the event sub-process—it is probably `Start2`.

11. Open Data Associations and map **orderNumber** and **orderStatus** from the **Order** process data object into **queryResult1**, as shown in the following screenshot:

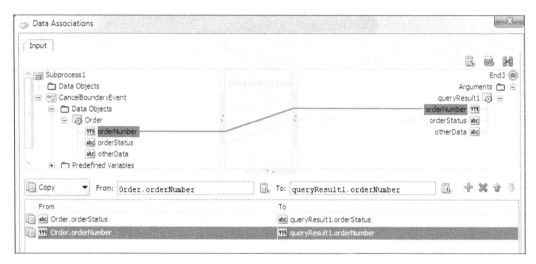

Now, we are ready to see our process in action:

12. Deploy the process to your server and select **New Revision ID** so that you do not overwrite your previous work.

13. Start a few instances of the process with different order numbers, for example, 11, 12, 13, and so on.

14. Send a query message for order number 12. Make sure you do this within one minute so that the process has not completed! To send this message you will need to change **Operation** to match the name of the **Start** node in the event sub-process — probably `start2`.

   You should get the message back almost immediately, with the order status as **STOCK ALLOCATED**, as shown in the following screenshot:

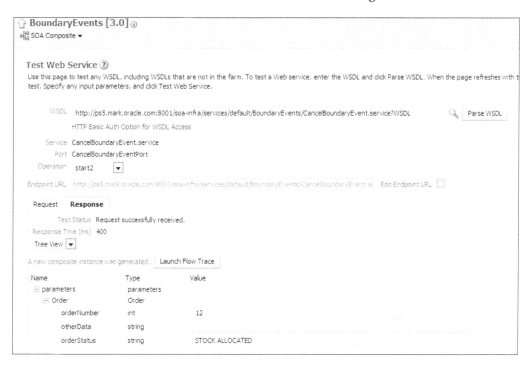

Now there are some problems with this approach. The big one is that it only works while the instance is running. What happens when the timer expires and your process moves on? Are you able to send a query message to see the ORDER PROCESSED status? You might like to go back and add another delay into your process so that you can in fact query both order statuses.

You might like to explore the audit trail a little as well. While the process instance is still running, you can see the details of the event sub-process in the audit trail. Can you see these details after the instance has completed?

Propagating exceptions using peer processes

In this practice, we will explore exception propagation. You may recall that exceptions are not automatically propagated from a peer process, which is invoked using a Throw Message Event back to the process that invoked it. Let's validate this behavior first and then update our processes so that we can catch and propagate the exception:

1. In JDeveloper, create a new **BPM Application** named **PropagatingExceptions**.

2. Create a **BPM Project** inside this named **PropagatingExceptions**.

3. Create a **Process** named **Process1**.

4. Into this process add an embedded sub-process (not an event sub-process).

5. In the sub-process add **Throw Message Event** and then **Catch Timer Event**.

6. Create a second **Process** named **Process2**.

7. In **Process2**, right click on the **End** node and change **Trigger Type** to **Error**. In the **Implementation** tab, click on the green plus icon to add new **Business Exception** named **BusinessException1**.

8. Save both processes.

9. Return to **Process1**. Open the **Implementation** tab for **Throw Message Event** and set **Type** to **Process Call**. Select **Process2** and set **Target Node** to **Start**.

10. Open the **Implementation** tab for **Catch Timer Event**. Set the timer to expire after one minute, as we did in the previous exercises.

    Your processes should now look similar to the following image, and we are ready to deploy and test.

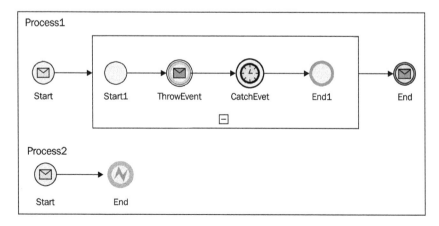

Run a test instance and observe what happens. You will notice that `Process1` continues running after `Process2` has suffered an exception and ended. `Process1` is never told what happened to `Process2`.

This is not what we wanted in this case. Let's update our processes now so that they work as we expect, and also `Process1` will be informed if `Process2` has an exception:

11. Return to **Process2** and add an event sub-process.

12. Open the **Implementation** tab for the **Start** node inside the event sub-process. Set **Implementation Type** to **Error** and check the options to catch all business and system exceptions. You could of course specify a particular exception, such as `BusinessException1`, but for now we want to catch any exceptions at all, as shown in the following screenshot:

13. Open the **Implementation** tab for the **End** node inside the event sub-process. Set **Implementation Type** to **Error**.

14. Set **Message Exchange** to **Define Interface** and choose **Default Conversation**.

Let's pause for a moment and make sure we understand what we have done here. We added an event sub-process to `Process2`, which will capture any type of exception—business or system. It will then send a message back to whoever called us (through the default conversation). This means that this process will no longer silently fail without the caller being notified.

Now, let's go back to `Process1` and catch this message:

1. In **Process1**, add a **Catch Message Event** boundary event to the embedded sub-process.

2. Open the **Implementation** tab for this boundary event and set **Message Exchange** to **Process Call**.

3. Set the **Process** to **Process2** and **Target Node** to **End1**.

4. Add **Terminate Event** to the process and wire the boundary event to this.

Your processes should now look similar to the following diagram, and we are ready to deploy and test.

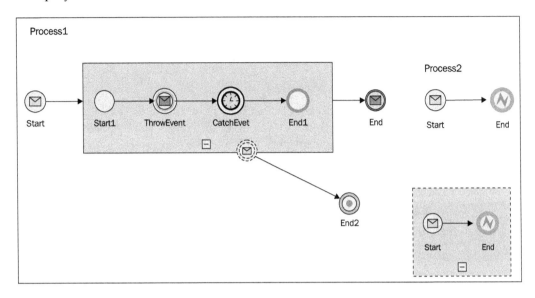

Test these new versions of the processes. You should now observe that the exception that occurs in Process2 is in fact propagated back to Process1.

You might like to experiment with defining different event sub-processes in Process2 to catch different kinds of exceptions. You might also like to experiment with adding some attributes to BusinessException1 so that you can pass some information about the exception back to the caller.

Summary

In this chapter, we have put into practice the theory we learned in the previous chapter about handling exceptions. We have explored the various mechanisms available for handling exceptions, including boundary events and event sub-processes. We have also explored the propagation of faults between processes.

Additionally, we have used some of the techniques we learned in earlier chapters, such as defining advanced conversations and correlation in order to create our practical examples.

We implemented two common patterns:

- The "cancel message" use case that lets us send a message to a running process instance to cancel it
- The "query" use case that lets us retrieve the value of process data objects from a running process instance

You are now armed with the theory and practical knowledge that you need to design quality BPMN processes that are able to communicate with each other safely, handle exceptions, and deal with data in arrays. Thank you for spending your time to learn with us!

Index

Symbols

(non-default) conversation 39

A

AddEmptyElement 60
arguments 22, 46
arrays
  creating, with some empty
      elements 57-60
  elements, appending to 62
  elements, getting from 62
  elements, removing from 63
  elements, setting from 62
  empty array, creating 53-56
  handling 51
  initialized array, creating 61
  iterating over, using an embedded
      sub-process 66-68
  iterating over, with a multi-instance
      embedded sub-process 63
  joining 63
asynchronous 8
Audit process 9
automatic correlation 11

B

boundary event
  about 70
  error 71
  interrupting 70
  message 71
  none 71
  non-interrupting 70
  signal 71
  timer 71
boundary events
  about 15
  used, for implementing cancel message use
      case 79-84
  used, for implementing timeouts 77-79
BPMN
  arrays, working with 51
  inter-process communication 7
  exception handling 69
  mechanisms for catching exceptions 70
business exceptions 69
business object 10

C

call activity 22
called process 12, 25
calling process
  about 25
  about 12
CancelBoundaryEvent process 84
cancel message use case
  implementing, boundary events
      used 79-84
cardinality 21
cardinality or collection 64
catch events 14
catch none event 22
collaboration diagram 8
collection 21

completion condition
  about 21, 65
  using 65
conversation
  about 8
  default conversation 10
correlation
  about 11, 25
  automatic correlation 11
  correlation set 11, 12
  keys 11
  message-based correlation 11
  multi-instance embedded
     sub-process 13, 14
correlation fault 11
correlation key 28
correlation set 11, 12
CreateEmptyArray 56

D

Data Association editor 52
Data Associations
  about 52
  expression 53
  XML Literal 53
  XSLT 53
default conversation 10

E

elements
  appending, to arrays 62
  getting, from arrays 62
  removing, from arrays 63
  setting, from arrays 62
embedded sub-process
  about 9, 19
  capabilities 20
empty array
  creating 53-56
empty elements
  used, for creating array 57-60
end (message) nodes 13
error, boundary events 71
errors 19

Event Delivery Network 18, 19
events or tasks use correlation 12
event sub-process
  about 9, 71, 72
  example 72
  using 84-87
exception
  about 69
  business exceptions 69
  system exceptions 69
exception handling 15
exception propagation
  sub-processes invoked with call activity 75
  with embedded sub-processes 73, 74
  with peer processes invoked with a send
     task 76
  with peer processes invoked with throw
     event 75
exceptions
  propagating, peer processes used 88-90

H

Handle Timeout activity 74

I

initialized array
  creating 61
inter-process communication
  about 7
  conversation 8
  correlation 11
  errors 19
  implementing, messages and correlation
     used 25-35
  inside loop 35-41
  message 18
  receive task 15
  send task 15
  signal 18
  signals, used 42-45
  throw and catch events 14
inter-process communication
  reusable sub-processes, using 45-48
interrupting boundary event 70

L

loop construct 11

M

mechanisms for catching exceptions
  boundary event 70
  event sub-process 71
message 18
message-based correlation 11, 12
message, boundary events 71
message catch events 13
mid-point receives 13
multi-instance embedded sub-process
  about 21, 64
  cardinality or collection 64
  characteristics 21, 64
  completion condition, using 65
  scope 65
  sequential or parallel 65
multi-instance sub-process 38
myconv1 9

N

node set 53
none, boundary events 71
non-interrupting boundary event 70

O

once and only once delivery 19
operation 52
operations, Data Association
  append 52
  copy 52
  copy list 52
  insert after 52
  insert before 52
Order Over Limit 9
orderStatus attribute 84

P

peer processes
  used, for propogating exceptions 88-90

peers 15
Process3 16
ProcessOrder process 9
publish/subscribe style communication 42

R

receive task 12, 15
recommended sub-process style 23
reusable sub-processes
  about 22, 45
  using 46-48
revision number 59

S

scope 65
scopeConv 9
scoped 9
scoped conversation 35, 38
scoped correlation key 39
send/receive tasks
  using 17
send task 13, 15
sequential or parallel 65
service contract 10
service task 15
signal 18
signal, boundary events 71
Something activity 73
sub-processes
  about 35
  embedded sub-process 20
  multi-instance embedded sub-processes 21
  recommended sub-process style 23
  reusable sub-processes 22
synchronous 8
system exceptions 69

T

throw/catch events
  using 17
throw events 14, 15
throw message event 9
throw none event 22

timeouts
    implementing, boundary events
        used 77-79
timer, boundary events 71
timer catch event 29

V

variables 46

W

WSDL port type 10

X

XML Literal 53
XPath function 53
XSLT 53

Thank you for buying
Oracle BPM Suite 11g: Advanced BPMN Topics

About Packt Publishing

Packt, pronounced 'packed', published its first book "*Mastering phpMyAdmin for Effective MySQL Management*" in April 2004 and subsequently continued to specialize in publishing highly focused books on specific technologies and solutions.

Our books and publications share the experiences of your fellow IT professionals in adapting and customizing today's systems, applications, and frameworks. Our solution-based books give you the knowledge and power to customize the software and technologies you're using to get the job done. Packt books are more specific and less general than the IT books you have seen in the past. Our unique business model allows us to bring you more focused information, giving you more of what you need to know, and less of what you don't.

Packt is a modern, yet unique publishing company, which focuses on producing quality, cutting-edge books for communities of developers, administrators, and newbies alike. For more information, please visit our website: www.PacktPub.com.

About Packt Enterprise

In 2010, Packt launched two new brands, Packt Enterprise and Packt Open Source, in order to continue its focus on specialization. This book is part of the Packt Enterprise brand, home to books published on enterprise software – software created by major vendors, including (but not limited to) IBM, Microsoft and Oracle, often for use in other corporations. Its titles will offer information relevant to a range of users of this software, including administrators, developers, architects, and end users.

Writing for Packt

We welcome all inquiries from people who are interested in authoring. Book proposals should be sent to author@packtpub.com. If your book idea is still at an early stage and you would like to discuss it first before writing a formal book proposal, contact us; one of our commissioning editors will get in touch with you.

We're not just looking for published authors; if you have strong technical skills but no writing experience, our experienced editors can help you develop a writing career, or simply get some additional reward for your expertise.

Getting Started With Oracle SOA Suite 11g R1 – A Hands-On Tutorial

ISBN: 978-1-847199-78-2   Paperback: 482 pages

Fast track your SOA adoption — Build a Service-Oriented composite Application in just hours!

1. Offers an accelerated learning path for the much anticipated Oracle SOA Suite 11g release

2. Beginning with a discussion of the evolution of SOA, this book sets the stage for your SOA learning experience

3. Includes a comprehensive overview of the Oracle SOA Suite 11g Product Architecture

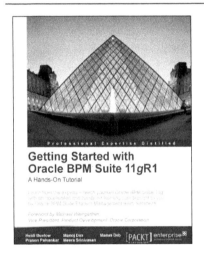

Getting Started with Oracle BPM Suite 11gR1 – A Hands-On Tutorial

ISBN: 978-1-849681-68-1   Paperback: 536 pages

Learn from the experts - teach yourself Oracle BPM Suite 11g with an accelerated and hands-on learning path brought yo you by Oracle BPM Suite Product Management team members

1. Offers an accelerated learning path for the much-anticipated Oracle BPM Suite 11g release

2. Set the stage for your BPM learning experience with a discussion into the evolution of BPM, and a comprehensive overview of the Oracle BPM Suite 11g Product Architecture

3. Discover BPMN 2.0 modeling, simulation, and implementation

Please check **www.PacktPub.com** for information on our titles

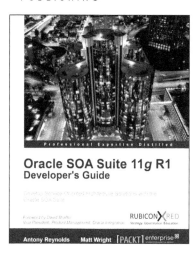

Oracle SOA Suite 11g R1 Developer's Guide

ISBN:978-1-849680-18-9   Paperback: 720 pages

Develop Service-Oriented Architecture Solutions with the Oracle SOA Suite

1. A hands-on, best-practice guide to using and applying the Oracle SOA Suite in the delivery of real-world SOA applications

2. Detailed coverage of the Oracle Service Bus, BPEL PM, Rules, Human Workflow, Event Delivery Network, and Business Activity Monitoring

3. Master the best way to use and combine each of these different components in the implementation of a SOA solution

Oracle BPM Suite 11g Developer's cookbook

ISBN: 978-1-849684-22-4   Paperback: 512 pages

Over 80 advanced recipes to develop rich, interactive business processes using the Oracle Business Process Management

1. Full of illustrations, diagrams, and tips with clear step-by-step instructions and real time examples to develop Industry Sample BPM Process and BPM interaction with SOA Components

2. Dive into lessons on Fault ,Performance and Rum Time Management

3. Explore User Interaction ,Deployment and Monitoring

4 Dive into BPM Process Implementation as process developer while conglomerating BPMN elements

Please check **www.PacktPub.com** for information on our titles